D1639666

Snarl for
the Camera

JAMES GRAY

Snarl for the Camera

Tales of a Wildlife Cameraman

PIATKUS

Copyright © 2002 by James Gray

First published in 2002 by
Judy Piatkus (Publishers) Limited
5 Windmill Street
London W1T 2JA
e-mail: info@piatkus.co.uk

The moral right of the author has been asserted

A catalogue record for this book is available from the British Library

ISBN 0-7499-2345-8

This book has been printed on paper manufactured with respect for the environment using wood from managed sustainable resources

Text design by Paul Saunders

Typeset by Phoenix Photosetting, Chatham, Kent
Printed and bound in Great Britain by
Mackays of Chatham Ltd, Chatham, Kent

Contents

Acknowledgements   vii

Prologue   1

1   Damsels, Distress and Success   4

2   The Serpent Beguiled Me   23

3   The Polar Bears' Picnic   41

4   It's Just Not Cricket   59

5   Catch a Caiman by its Tail   68

6   Protective Custody   81

7   The Great Call of The Wild   95

8   I Counted Them All Out and I Counted Them All Back In Again   109

9   Little Brown Jobs   118

10   A Recipe for Scrambled Eggs   132

11   Gorilla Tactics   143

12   Weasel Words   153

SNARL FOR THE CAMERA

13	Bamboo and Beer	164
14	I Know a Hawk from a Handsaw	171
15	Cold Comfort	181
16	There's Gold in Them There Hills	209
17	Hovering on the Edge of Insanity	218
18	Castaway	229
19	Life, Death and Taxes	242
	Afterword	270

Acknowledgements

The first group of people I would like to thank is the band of long-suffering assistants who have worked with me over the years. I have referred to several of them in this book, but I have not given an adequate picture of how much I owe them. These debts range from creating a few good meals to saving my life. So I would like to thank (in alphabetical order) Chris Barker, Tim Borrill, Chris Catton, Jane-Maire Franklyn, Philip Lovel, William Moult and Jason Roberts. Strangely absent from the book is Tony Allen, who has been my filming partner for many years. He is a cameraman like myself so we shared very few field adventures once we both became established, but I would like to thank him for his quiet support.

In relation to the book itself, I would like to thank my agent Kate Hordern, Broo Doherty, Angela Blackburn and Liz Robinson who all helped with the script, and Alan Brooke of Piatkus whose editing has been invaluable.

*This book is dedicated to my wife Caroline
and my daughters Emma and Kate*

Prologue

I T WAS ONE OF THOSE RARE and beautiful moments, and it brought me something of a revelation. As moments go, it might not have been to everybody's taste, but it was my moment, and I thought it was damn near perfect. It came while I was sitting on a hillside in the Abruzzi Mountains of central Italy and that skyline of craggy peaks makes an ideal backdrop for a revelation. In front of me stood my camera with my biggest telephoto lens on the front of it. When I peered down the viewfinder I could just about make out something large and dark being swallowed by the gathering dusk. Having watched it all day, I knew I was looking at the carcass of a cow that the park authorities had dragged there the evening before. I was there with the sole purpose of filming the gourmets this tasty morsel was intended for. Bears.

The bears of the Abruzzi are some of the few surviving brown bears in Western Europe, and they are well protected. The autumn feeding regime was introduced some time ago so as to ensure that the bears can go into hibernation fat enough to sleep right through till spring. The park authorities also hope that by putting out food, the wolves that are the other great boast of the park might not kill quite so many sheep on the nearby farms. Personally, I would have been thrilled to film a wolf or two feeding on my dead cow because I love wolves, but the bears were what we were really after.

Shortly after I had settled in, the sun came up over my right shoulder, and I watched it all day as it travelled across an immaculate blue sky. All day I sat on those rocks and they became harder, sharper and lumpier by the hour. All day I gazed at the carcass, willing a bear to appear. The morning's excitement had been a fox that came and tried to eat a bit of cow, but it was clearly out of its league. That was about it for the morning and the afternoon was slightly less eventful, so by evening I had to recognise that I was not going to film a bear that day. But then, just as the sun finally set, a thin crescent moon rose. I was gazing at the moon when my moment came. Unannounced, the wolves started howling. Their glorious greeting to the new moon echoed round the mountains and sent a shiver of excitement and fear down my spine.

And the revelation? When the wolves finally stopped their chorus, the reality of the situation struck me. I am a professional wildlife cameraman. My job is to bring back the best possible images of the wild for the TV screens of the world. But the best times, the pure champagne moments, the nuggets that will live with me till I die, rarely end up on film. Time and again it seems to be too dark, or the animal is too far away or too close or something like a rock obscures the action. For any one of a dozen reasons, the very best experiences are no more than images in my head, and I decided to write this book so as to share some of them.

CHAPTER ONE

Damsels, Distress and Success

I N A LEAFY OUTER-LONDON SUBURB, a boy lay on his bed. He was about twelve years old, and he lay on his back watching a man. The man had fair hair roughly like the boy's, but there the similarity ended. The boy was rather over-weight, and his friends at school called him 'Tubby', but the man was tall, lean and tanned. In fact, as the boy watched him, the man seemed to become a little taller and leaner.

The man stood up and now the boy could see that he was wearing boots with khaki shorts and a bush shirt. He picked up his hat and a rifle before he walked out of the tent. His eyes scanned the familiar skyline where he could make out the crater of Ngoro-goro, Mount Kilimanjaro, the Serengeti and all the lakes of the East African rift valley. As far as the eye could see the plains swarmed with game – wildebeest, elephant, zebra, giraffe, buffalo, and he knew there were lions out there too. Today he was after the lions, but as he took his binoculars from the camp table, his beautiful wife came up to him.

'Do be careful James,' she said.

'I'm always careful darling,' he replied. 'All I need is one shot, and I'm going to get it today.'

He walked over to his Land Rover, checked his film gear and climbed in. As he drove off, the boy heard a familiar voice.

'Supper's ready James,' shouted my mother. 'Come on down and don't forget to wash your hands.'

I am not sure when I started dreaming about becoming a wildlife cameraman, but I devoted hours and years of my childhood to my fantasy. Much of the rest of my time I devoted to studying first natural history and then, more formally, biology. I was fascinated by the subject, and it all became part of my plan to become a cameraman.

After school and a degree in zoology, I joined a very select band: those who read the credits at the end of TV programmes. I was of course watching all the wildlife programmes, and with time, one name came to stand out from the others. The credit was as 'Executive Producer' for a series of BBC programmes that I particularly liked. The series was called *Private Lives*, and the producer's name was Jeffrey Boswell.

With the brashness of youth, I phoned him and explained that I wanted to be a wildlife cameraman. I told him all about my degree, my fascination with wildlife and my lifelong yearning to do the job. I never did discover why Jeffrey took me seriously, but right from the start he did.

I kept pestering him till, one day, he revealed that there were lots of young people who wanted to be wildlife cameramen. I was stunned. It had always seemed such an unlikely ambition that I had never realised I shared it with anybody.

As if that wasn't enough, Jeffrey went on. 'So James, what makes you different from all the others?'

I spluttered for a while till he said, 'If you want to be a wildlife cameraman, you'd better get yourself a camera. Go and film something. Then we can look at what you've shot, and we'd have something to talk about.'

By this stage I was working in North Wales at a field centre, teaching biology to a steady stream of students. The field centre was right next to the River Conway, so I decided to make a film about the Conway Estuary. I bought a camera and a couple of lenses. The camera cost me £100 and the lenses £50 and £75 respectively. I borrowed more lenses and a tripod. I made myself a hide from an old tent and devoted my free time for the next year to filming everything I could on the estuary.

The first time I used my hide might well have been the last because I nearly got myself arrested. An eager local policeman had spotted this strange tent out on the mud, and decided that I was a member of the IRA checking out Conway Bridge so as to blow it up. I managed to convince him that I was a harmless eccentric, and he in turn revealed himself to be addicted to wildlife programmes so he wished me luck and left me in peace. I have used the 'harmless eccentric' tactic frequently since then and it almost always works; perhaps it contains a grain of truth.

Mine was of course to be the definitive programme about the estuary, so it had to include more things than just birds. I began delving into the less familiar parts of the animal kingdom with a worm. It was a handsome red worm, about twenty centimetres long and very keen on burrowing. So I set up the camera on my tripod and pointed it at the worm. It looked awful. All I could see was black mud with a thin red line running across it like a road on a map. I caught the worm again and put it back into its jam-jar while I rearranged the camera. This time I had the camera on a piece of plastic laid on the mud so that I was looking almost horizontal. That looked much better, but my worm still looked a bit insignificant in the shot.

I tried all kinds of things, and worked out that the lower I got the camera the better the shot looked. I reasoned that if I could get the lens right down till it was level with the surface of the mud, my worm would look great. So I dug a hole for the camera to go in. That involved a ridiculous amount of floundering about because, as I discovered, estuary mud is slimy, deep and very sticky.

When eventually I had my hole to my liking, I lined it with polythene and carefully lowered my beloved camera into it. This left me with one small problem. I had to look through the viewfinder, and it was at mud level. In my eagerness to protect my camera, I had used all my polythene, which meant that I had to lie face down in the mud.

My first impression was that estuary mud is soft and remarkably comfortable to lie in. However, as the slime oozed through my shirt and trousers, I realised that it is also cold, wet and stinking. That mud proved to have an incomparable ability to spread itself across anybody stupid enough to lie in it. Almost imperceptibly I sank into the ooze. Face, hands, hair, clothes; everything was caked in the stuff. I ended up looking like an over-eager military cadet on a camouflage training course. If my policeman had found me then I would have had no chance.

The good news was that for that brief muddy moment when I looked through the viewfinder, the worm looked superb. But I decided that I had had enough of lying in foul sticky mud: I was going to cheat. I would take my worm back to the centre, and film it in the lab there. That worm was followed by a series of weird and wonderful animals that I dredged from the estuary. I filmed them all in the lab, but obviously if I wanted to make them look at all realistic, I had to film them with a background of mud. So it became the summer of mud. I carried bucket after bucket of the malodorous stuff into the lab. Mud took over my life, and insidiously it spread through the centre. The smell came to dominate the place. The other staff kept apologising to the students, but I was undeterred.

Quite early on, I decided that my film had to include people as well as animals because I wanted to show how we were affecting the habitat. So in addition to the wildlife, I filmed roads clogged with cars and sewers spewing out filth. I filmed tourists on the sand and discovered that people behave in extraordinary ways when a camera is pointed at them. I had to resort to all sorts of subterfuge to film people behaving normally. So I lurked behind rubbish bins and peered round wind-breaks. I expected to be arrested at any moment and have charges as a voyeur added to my burgeoning criminal record, but somehow I got away with it.

The camera I was using was a wind-up Bolex, and I loved it dearly. They are wonderfully robust and reliable things and just about the most basic cameras that can shoot the 16mm film that is needed for television screening. Mine could only take hundred foot rolls of film, which last about three minutes each, but I rarely shot as much as a whole roll in a day's filming. Today I often shoot a thousand feet in a day. There is one small but significant difference: I was paying for everything myself out of a rather meagre salary. This imposed a discipline that not only made me parsimonious with film; it also made me plan very carefully what I was going to do.

I watched the wildlife programmes on television even more intently than before, trying desperately to work out how they were made. I bought books on film technique and read up about film grammar. I read that you need wide shots, tight shots and details, but when I tried to do this, my precious film just flashed through the camera. For each subject I started with the tightest shots. They are generally the most difficult and if they proved impossible, there was no point in getting the wide shots: they would be no use without the close-ups, so shooting them would just waste precious film. I planned sequences, and made myself shot lists that I stuck to like chewing gum.

When I left the field centre a year later, I spent two months editing my film, and that was a sobering experience. Trying to put one shot after another showed me why the books all bang on about the rules of film grammar.

'You should cut from one shot to the next as the subject of the shot moves. The subject must be of different sizes in the two shots.'

Trying to edit my footage, I could suddenly see what worked and what didn't, and the rules became less arbitrary. I eventually managed to string together a ten-minute film about the Conway Estuary and the way that tourism threatens it. I also came to the conclusion that the best way to learn to be a cameraman is to try editing your own footage.

When I phoned Jeffrey Boswell again it must have been eighteen months since we had last spoken. Either he has a phenomenal memory, or he is a consummate bluffer, because I had the definite impression that he remembered me. I came straight to the point.

'I've made a film.'

'Excellent dear boy.' He really does talk like that. 'Bring it down to Bristol and we can have a look at it.'

So we fixed a date and I found myself walking into the BBC with a film can under my arm. I felt ten feet tall, till it came to watching my efforts with a BBC Series Editor sitting next to me. This was rather different from sitting watching it with Caroline, who had recently become my wife. Suddenly all the shortcomings became glaring disasters. I found myself mumbling apologies and excuses as we went on. Ten minutes is a long time to be embarrassed.

'Well,' said Jeffrey, when at last the torture stopped, 'that's not bad. You've learned a lot.' He broke it to me gently that it was not the sort of thing he could use in his series, '. . . but you do have the makings of a cameraman,' he added as consolation.

Then we went through the whole thing once more, this time with Jeffrey stopping again and again to ask me what I was trying to do, what was wrong with this shot or what shot should have come next. It was the first tutorial I had had since I left university, and I realised that I had a lot to learn.

'So where do we go from here?' asked Jeffrey when we got to the end.

I knew just where I wanted to go, but for once kept quiet about lions and East Africa. Instead I mumbled something about needing his advice.

'I'll tell you what,' he went on. 'If you can come up with a proposal for a programme that I like, I will see what I can do to help you make it.' That seemed like an offer of the keys to heaven, and I simply beamed back at him. He added that there was no way he could offer me a proper contract but he would try to help me get into the business.

Private Lives, the series that Jeffrey was responsible for at the time consisted of half-hour programmes, each of which was about a single species. He went on to give me a few clues about the type of subject he might go for.

'The first trick is to pick the right animal and I've got a golden rule about what makes a successful programme for my series. You have to be able to tell me thirteen interesting things about the animal you pick. It's a magic number. With thirteen topics we can tell the viewer something new every two minutes, and that's about right.'

Having a vaguely mathematical mind, I queried Jeffrey's multiplication, so he explained that a TV half-hour is only twenty-six minutes long. That allows for titles, credits, adverts and trailers for the next programme but one. So I was aiming at a twenty-six-minute programme about something.

My brain was doing thirteen to the dozen. What animals were there that I could tell you three interesting things about, let alone thirteen? Lions of course, but there had been several films about them. What about gorillas? They're amazing. Easily think of thirteen things about them. Eye gestures. Social groups. Parental care. But how could I film them? Jeffrey was coming up with more gold.

'The thing at this stage is to find something that you can work on from home,' he said. 'That way you can really put in the time, and believe me, the only way to make a decent wildlife film is for the cameraman to spend time with the animals.'

That rather ruled out gorillas. Shame, but if I had heard him aright, Jeffrey Boswell had just referred to me as a cam-man. This was not the moment to give up. How about dogs, fallow deer, mice. Being based at home still left ds of animals. But what would work?

'Here. Let me give you some old treatments.' He was handing me a stack of papers. 'These were the proposals for some of the programmes that went out at the beginning of the year. If you want to have a go at this, you'll have to send me something along these lines. Give me a ring if you come up with an idea. Talk to me about it first rather than spend ages on something we're doing already. Give me a ring.'

I walked along Whiteladies Road outside the BBC with my head spinning. I just had to come up with something and it had to be good.

About a week later, Caroline and I happened to go sailing on one of the gravel pits near Oxford where we lived. It was a lovely warm summer day so between races I wandered off casually bird-watching among the gravel workings, and there, over the little ponds left behind by the digging I noticed little wisps of blue smoke. As I got closer, the smoke materialised into diminutive dragonflies, known as damselflies, and there were swarms of them hovering over the shallow water. I was entranced by their beauty, and amazed by the sheer numbers of the things. A single damselfly is attractive but clouds of them are mesmerising. I missed the next race watching them, but it dawned on me that they might just meet Jeffrey's criteria for a film.

For a start, these little creatures were close to home so Jeffrey's first point was safely met. They were also easy to find, which had to be a plus point if I was going to film them. More importantly, they were so beautiful that I had just spent a happy half-hour watching them. Grudgingly I admitted to myself that I have spent many happy half-hours watching animals that other people seem to find boring, but there was no denying that these damselflies were both beautiful and fascinating. I had yet to hit the magic thirteen points but damselflies seemed like contenders.

When I got home I quickly worked out that the species I had been looking at was the Common Blue Damselfly. As names go 'Common Blue Damselfly' is not that sexy, but it is remarkably accurate. The males are a dazzling blue even if the females are a rather dull khaki, and 'Common' suggested two things to me. For a start they should be easy to find, but more importantly I reasoned that there should be plenty of information about them.

Once I had the identification sorted out I started looking in all my natural history and biology books to find out more about these little creatures. That yielded something but not enough, so over the next few weeks I tracked down more books on the subject, and managed to find my old reader's ticket for the Bodlean Library in Oxford where I discovered much more about them. As a subject for a film, they just got better the more I read. Within a couple of weeks I had confidently hit the magic number of thirteen and tentatively listed seventeen amazing facts. I liked the idea of a safety margin since one or two of my facts did seem a bit hard to film.

I phoned Jeffrey again and exploded with enthusiasm at him.

'Yes, yes James. Now put it down on paper the way I showed you and I will have a look at it all.'

So I hauled out my old typewriter and started hammering out the first of the many programme treatments that I would write over the years. Down the left side I listed the intended shots, and in the right hand column I put the ideas that would make up the commentary. I included all the stuff I had learned about damselflies, all the shots I hoped to film and all the fascinating facts I could add.

My list of amazing facts read roughly as follows:

Introduction and ancestry
Damselflies are some of the most ancient of insects. Their ancestors have been found as fossils alongside dinosaurs in the coal measures of the Carboniferous era. The chief difference is that the ancient forms were much bigger than the present day species, so some of the dragonflies had a wingspan of over seventy-five centimetres.

Courtship
Damselfly courtship is brief. The male catches the female by her head or thorax, using his legs. He then switches to holding her with special claspers at the tip of his abdomen. These claspers fit into notches in the front of her thorax. They fly about in this tandem position looking for a suitable place to mate.

Mating
The pair settles in the vegetation near the pond to mate. The male hangs onto the female with his claspers throughout the mating. First, the male smears some sperm onto a special organ on the ventral side of his abdomen. Then the

female loops round to collect the sperm, so the pair takes up a wheel position.

Egg-laying sites

Once they have mated, the pair resumes the tandem position and flies off to the pond so that the female can lay her eggs on the pondweed. As they hunt for a suitable egg-laying site, the pair is harried mercilessly by other males.

Egg-laying

For the female to lay her eggs, the pair must settle on a bit of weed at the surface. The female then crawls down the weed going fully under water. As she crawls down the stem, her mate at last releases his grip of her thorax but remains hovering above her.

Underwater egg-laying

She cuts a series of tiny notches in the plant with a spike on the tip of her abdomen and inserts a single egg into each of these holes. The eggs are a less than a millimetre long. She may stay underwater for half an hour or so, laying dozens of eggs.

Air–sea rescue

When she surfaces, a male grabs her immediately. Thousands of males hover above laying sites waiting for the chance to catch surfacing females. Once a male is holding a female firmly, he takes her off to mate again in the bushes. Females that are not lifted out of the water quickly may fall prey to fish.

Egg hatching
After about three weeks, a pro-larva emerges from the egg
and as soon as it is sticking through the surface of the plant,
it moults again into the first true larval stage.

Larvae
A larva is a miniature dragon that stalks our ponds and
lakes. It has three blade-like gills at the tip of its abdomen:
these gills are for absorption of oxygen, and also act as a tail
for swimming, but though they swim well, larvae spend
much of their time lurking in the vegetation.

Larval feeding
The larvae are carnivorous, eating things like water fleas
and midge larvae, which they catch with a hydraulically
operated jaw. This jaw unfolds forwards to catch prey as
much as a centimetre in front of the animal.

Cannibalism
When larvae become really common in a pond, they may
become cannibalistic.

Fish predation
In spring, larvae swim to the edge of their pond to metamorphose into adults, but in doing so they become easy
prey for fish.

Emergence
Larvae usually emerge at dawn, and do so by crawling up

the stem of a plant into the air. When they metamorphose, the dorsal side of the thorax splits, and out comes the adult. The wings inflate as 'blood' is pumped into them. They then harden off, so the adult can fly about two hours after the larva crawled out of the water.

Young adults
Young adults fly rather weakly, so they are vulnerable, but their wings become fully functional within a few days.

Wings and flying
In flight a damselfly moves its two pairs of wings independently, and this enables it to hover.

Adult feeding
Adult damselflies feed by catching insects on the wing, but they usually settle to chew up what they catch.

A new generation
Damselflies mature within a few days and develop their adult colouring at about that time, so they are then ready to mate and complete the cycle.

I was rather impressed. I had a safety margin of four items, and I reckoned that most of my points would be filmable, though there were one or two that I was worried about. I also had very little idea how much screen time each of my topics would fill. Some of them, such as the male catching the female, would hardly take more than a few seconds, but others, such as the egg-laying, could go on for ages. I just hoped that the extra four topics would make the total long enough for the half-hour.

I sent the completed document to Jeffrey and held my breath. A couple of days later I had a phone call.

'Yes, James. Damselflies could work as an idea. Mind you, we hardly ever have insect programmes. They're just not as spectacular as mammals, but this is interesting. Not easy to film, mind. Leave it with me and I'll see what I can do to help you.'

I was bowled over, and started having fantasies about actually becoming a cameraman, and going on a field maintenance course for Land Rovers. He came back to me a week or so later.

'I've found a way to help you, but it's modest. I can let you have three thousand feet of film plus processing. I've managed to save it on another project, so I can put it through the accounts under that heading. All I ask for is first refusal on the finished programme. What do you say?'

For a while I could say nothing. What he called modest seemed like boundless generosity to me. He was offering me film plus processing. He had mentioned three thousand feet – that was more than I had used on the whole Conway project, and he wanted first refusal. When at last my stammering became coherent I let Jeffrey know that I would be delighted to accept his offer. So he put the deal down in a letter, and sent me the film. I had a programme to make.

Filming damselflies used all the skills, tricks and understanding I had gleaned while filming the estuary, and then some. Friends who came to stay had to share our spare bedroom with half a dozen tanks plus all the tripods and lights that I had assembled so as to film the larvae underwater. During that summer, I spent days up to my neck in a pond with the tripod and camera just above the water level in an attempt to get interesting shots of adults hovering above the water. On one such occasion a grass snake swam right between my legs as it hunted for frogs. Another time, a little vole swam across the pond towards me and proceeded to sit on my protruding knee, drying himself for a couple of minutes. I was enjoying the reality of filming as much as my fantasies had led me to hope.

Filming the female laying her eggs was a problem, but, after numerous failures, I discovered that if I caught a pair that had just mated, the female would remain in egg-laying mode for some time. So I took a tank with me to the pond, and put a female onto a piece of pondweed in the tank. She immediately obliged and crawled down the weed to lay her eggs in a stem right next to the glass of the tank. With a bit of trial and error, I got this set up right and managed to film her egg-laying under water.

Then of course, I wanted to get the extreme tight shot of her cutting into the pondweed with the little dagger on the tip of her abdomen and inserting her egg into the plant. So I replaced the pondweed in my tank with a strip of cucumber and put a female on it. Cucumber is virtually transparent, so I could see and film the egg being injected into the plant.

After filming for a year I knew I had nothing like all I needed for a programme, so I told Jeffrey that I would need another year. His reaction was gently supportive, but he let it be known that there was no more film coming my way for a while. So it was back to buying my own film-stock and using it as sparingly as possible.

I had one supreme bit of good luck, and that came when I decided to try and film the egg hatching. Damselfly eggs are tiny, you could probably get half a dozen onto a pinhead, so over the summer holidays I managed to borrow a microscope from the school where I had a job as a biology teacher. I bought an adapter to fit the camera onto the microscope, and on the first day of the holidays, I set it all up on the dining room table just to try it out. I put a piece of pondweed under the microscope and had a look through the viewfinder. It was quite easy to see the damselfly eggs, and inside one of them I could just see the embryonic larva moving about, so I loaded up the camera, and snatched a few shots of the embryo. To my amazement it turned out to be a pro-larva, and it proceeded to break its way through its egg case and hatch. The entire process took about a minute and I managed to film it all. I had never before seen a damselfly hatch, and I have never seen it since, but I had it on film. I put the microscope away and got on with the rest of the story.

When eventually I decided that I had finished filming, I realised I was stuck again. What was I to do with it next? I couldn't believe that anybody would be able to look at the uncut film and visualise the finished programme in all that mess. I could, but I knew each frame intimately. I had filmed about three times as much footage as Jeffrey had given me, so I had about nine thousand feet of film, and just looking at that much would be a major undertaking. At normal speed it would take about four-and-a-half hours. I told myself that nobody would be able to look at all that and see the programme that was hiding amongst all the rubbish. Anyway I'd made so many mistakes that a lot of it was too embarrassing to show anybody in the business.

So I decided to edit it. A simple decision, but it took months to do. This was partly because editing always is a very slow process, and partly because I still had a proper job as a schoolteacher, so I could only edit during weekends and holidays. Fully four years after I had started on the project, I had something that I thought I could show to people. It wasn't finally edited: I had just put it together so as to show that it could tell the story.

Obviously the first person to see it had to be Jeffrey. He had wanted first refusal on the programme, and he was the first to refuse it.

'No dear boy, I am sorry but it just doesn't quite have the punch we need for a prime time programme. You've done an impressive job, but I am afraid I can't use it.'

That was a dark day, and it was several weeks before I could rekindle my spirits enough to do anything more about the thing. But then I phoned up Survival Anglia, and spoke to a producer there. Could I come up to London and show him what I had done?

So three days later I heard those memorable words 'Yes, I like it. We'll buy it.' And I realised that my career as a cameraman had started.

CHAPTER TWO

The Serpent Beguiled Me

THE GAP BETWEEN MY CHILDHOOD dreams and the reality of being a wildlife cameraman had rarely seemed so great. I had dreamt of driving across the sun-drenched plains of East Africa: what I was actually doing was wallowing knee-deep in the biggest area of swamp I had ever seen. The weed was clinging to my bare legs and with each step bubbles of foetid marsh gas crept up my thighs. The stinking, slimy muck I was pushing my way through made the Conway Estuary seem positively friendly. This new patch of mud was part of the flood plain of the Orinoco River in Venezuela, and I was having serious doubts about what on earth I was doing there.

I wasn't alone in my folly; ten metres to my left Chris, my assistant, was floundering along like me. Ten metres to my right, Maria was also picking her way through the slime. Each one of us had a long stick and we were all pushing these sticks into the mud in front of ourselves as we went along and it struck me that sensible people don't do things like that.

Maria was about the only encouraging thing about our crazy situation. She was pretty, petite and a world expert on the local reptiles. She seemed sensible enough, or she did if you overlooked her tendency to wade through swamps. So I thought I would briefly check with her about the hazards of what we were doing.

'Maria. Is it dangerous, wading in this swamp?' I asked her. The dangers I was thinking of were principally the diseases, infections and parasites that stagnant water harbours, especially in the tropics. Bilharzia, cholera and tetanus were on my mind – and those were just the ones I had heard of.

'No,' said Maria as she prodded the slime with her stick. 'Not really,' she added between prods. 'Piranhas,' she went on, 'No problem.' Prod. 'They are usually in open water.'

This came as good news and bad. The good part was that what we were standing in could never be described as open water. The bad part was that I hadn't realised that there were piranhas in the area in the first place, and it's a bit of a mixed blessing being reassured over something you aren't worrying about – especially when there were plenty of other things you are worrying about. Then as I waded on, I was struck by one small detail of what Maria had said: 'Piranhas are *usually* in open water.' 'What about slightly eccentric piranhas?' I asked myself. They probably bite like their conventional cousins. 'Don't think about it,' I told myself. I was about to press Maria on the subject of cholera and so on when she came up with more reassurance.

'There are not many leeches.'

Good, I said to myself. But then again, it doesn't take many leeches to make life miserable.

'And caiman,' she went on, 'if you hit one with your stick,' here she prodded the swamp with extra vigour, 'it will run away.'

I knew a bit about caiman because we were going to film them later and I had read up about them before I left home. They are the South American alligator and despite my reading, I hadn't expected to find them in the swamps. I thought that they stuck to the open water (like the piranhas). So they would run away if we hit them with our sticks would they? What if we missed one with our sticks and trod on it? My worries hung over me as I ploughed ahead.

Throughout this spasmodic conversation Maria waded on and prodded the slime with her stick, so I felt morally obliged to stay with her and do the same. What neither of us had thought to mention were the creatures we were actually looking for in this vast bog. There I really did need reassurance but I knew I wasn't likely to get any. I tried not to think about them too much though, because we were looking for anacondas, and anacondas come quite high up my private list of 'creatures that you don't really want to bump into unannounced'.

My mind kept dwelling on the things that my literature search had told me about anacondas before I left home. For a start they are the biggest snakes in the world, and although there is some doubt just how big they can grow, nine metres is often quoted as the longest and that is enormous. Records over eight metres are probably unreliable, but even the thought of a snake that big is alarming. Nineteenth-century travellers' tales go even bigger than that with accounts of snakes forty or fifty feet (twelve to fifteen metres) long but they really do seem to be exaggerations. Those accounts came from early visitors to the Orinoco marshes, so we were in the best possible place to bump into the biggest snakes in the world. That was why I was there, so there was no point in complaining about it.

Anacondas put their size to good effect when it comes to killing their prey. Like most of the really big snakes they kill by constricting, which means that they coil around their unfortunate victim and squeeze it to death. Then they swallow their prey whole. Small anacondas eat things like rats and wading birds, but big ones live on things like pigs and deer. There have been numerous records of them killing people.

We were looking for the biggest snakes in the world, and we were in one of their strongholds. Maria had told us enthusiastically about her research, and had assured us that there were tens of thousands of anacondas in the region. She went on to tell us that the exact area she had taken us to was home to the very biggest ones. Anacondas lurk in marshes, and live by catching animals that wade in the shallows. We were wading in the shallows. Big ones can kill people. Great.

I looked again at Maria for consolation. She was a few metres from me, squelching along, knee-deep in slime, prodding her long stick into the marsh in front of her and apparently she was unafraid. Gender stereotyping told me that anacondas couldn't be all that dangerous, so I floundered on.

When we had started looking for snakes, Maria had told us what would happen. 'When you hit a snake with your stick you see the plants move.' I was watching the waterweed the way a cat watches a mouse hole. I didn't want to miss the big moment and accidentally walk on any snake that I had managed to annoy by prodding it with a stick.

Maria covered that possibility as well. 'If you are lucky and tread on one, you feel it with your feet.' That reminded me vaguely of Clint Eastwood saying in one of his films, 'How lucky d'ya feel, punk?' As I recall, he had a gun pushed half way up the nose of the man he was talking to, and I felt for that punk as I waded on.

Maria's other comment before we launched ourselves into the ooze was even more inscrutable than the stuff about walking on anacondas or the usual habits of piranhas. She asked me to bring a sock with me. She offered no explanation, just 'please bring a sock'. So, armed with one sock, my trusty stick and a head-full of rather alarming zoological knowledge I confidently waded through the marsh hunting for anacondas.

That confidence proved a house of cards as soon as Maria found a snake.

'First, we find its head,' she said. No, first we run away. She had found this shiny, grey, moving thing about the diametre of my forearm.

'How?'

'Pull bits of snake out of the water like this with your stick. The head will come out.'

'But we can't do anything even if we manage to see its head,' I spluttered. 'We can't film it here.' Even to me, this sounded pathetic, but that snake was a very alarming sight. I'm not particularly frightened of snakes, but this thing was big, and I knew that anacondas have a well-earned reputation as animals not to mess with.

'We catch it and take it to where we can film it.' Did she say catch it? Her English wasn't that good, so maybe this was a mistake in translation, but there was no time to pursue the subject.

'There's the head. Where's the tail?' As Maria said this, something appeared from the slime, and it was horrible. Mesmerised, I watched a huge malignant mouth materialise suddenly from the swamp. That mouth was made up of soft puffy pallid skin ringed with thousands of teeth. It struck at Maria's stick. Even looking at it made my head spin. If I'd known there were things like that around, I would never have gone wading in these swamps.

My reaction was ridiculous because it wasn't as though this was the first snake I had met. I had worked with quite a few over the years, and thought I was comfortable with them. I had filmed rattlesnakes in America, and that had included getting them to strike straight at the camera.

When I had filmed garter snakes in Canada I had had to climb into a pit with an estimated twelve thousand snakes as they emerged from hibernation. They are quite small snakes, and non-venomous, but it would have been a testing experience for somebody who was frightened of snakes. I had even filmed a king cobra and had a rather narrow squeak when I found myself face to face with it.

But that mouth appearing from nowhere stopped me in my tracks. Somehow I had always thought of venomous snakes as being the ones that strike, and anacondas are non-venomous. So what was it doing striking like that? Anacondas constrict, I told myself, but this monster brought home to me a fact that I had never really faced: a constrictor has to get hold of its victim with its teeth while it wraps those famous coils around it. Otherwise the animal would run away.

While I was hypnotised by the head, Maria had found the tail. It was quite a long way from the head and this seemed like more bad news as it told of a big snake, but that distance became a boon with Maria's next command.

'We all catch the tail, and pull it out of the water onto the grass.' The only good thing about this was that we would be operating about three metres from all those teeth.

'What's to stop it turning round and going for us?' I asked.

'It can't reach so far. When it is straight it can't strike at all.' Easy. So we all grabbed the tail, pulled it out straight and dragged it onto a drier spot.

'Chris, you hold the tail. I catch its head, and James, you

help me.' I had no time to work out what this could mean, because suddenly Maria imitated the action of a mongoose. There was none of the stiffening the sinews and summoning up the blood for her, she dived straight onto the animal's head, and caught it with both hands, closing that dreadful mouth as she did so. Chris was pulling the tail for all he was worth.

'James get that coil off my arm.' It was like untangling a fire hose, but a fire hose with enormous strength and a big attitude problem. I pulled coils off her arms and legs but out of nowhere the snake had thrown a couple of coils around my arm locking Maria and me together. Under normal circumstances that would have had its attractions, but my mind was on other things. I managed to disentangle myself, and set about freeing Maria again. I pulled a succession of coils off Maria's arms and legs, but soon even I could see that we were winning. Reptiles generally have rather poor stamina and this snake was visibly tiring.

'The sock,' said Maria once she was properly free. With a flourish, I produced my slightly dirty Argyle cotton/nylon sock, and held it open for Maria carefully to push the creature's head into it. Almost immediately the snake stopped its writhing and we taped the sock closed. At last we could put it down and get a proper look at it. It was huge. Over three metres long, its middle was fatter than my calf. It had a lovely dark orange pattern at the head end, and along its length the scales glistened beautifully.

Once I had adjusted to the idea of anacondas striking, the squeezing business was what interested me most. The surprise was that it hadn't squeezed all that tightly. I had expected to be gripped in a vice, but it was more like the armband that my doctor uses as an excuse to tell me that my blood pressure is too high. That would be enough to crush a wading bird like a heron, but I told myself that my ribs could take pressure like that. What I conveniently forgot for the moment was the fact that once it gets a few coils wrapped round a large animal's body, an anaconda waits for its victim to breathe out. Instantly the coils take up the slack and breathing in becomes impossible. Most large victims die from suffocation.

'A nice little male,' said Maria interrupting my morbid thoughts. Not one word of her statement rang true.

'How can you tell what sex it is?' asked Chris.

'It is small so I think it has to be male.' This comment silenced both Chris and myself.

Maria confirmed her guess by examining the snake carefully. Snakes only have one opening at the back end of the body unlike the two that mammals have, so everything goes through the same hole, called a cloaca. The usual way to determine the sex of a snake is to examine its cloaca, and like most snakes, male and female anacondas have different patterns of scales in that area. These differences relate to the animal's sex organs and the details that you have to look for depend on the species. I had made a note of the specific features of anacondas before I left home, but Maria had first hand experience of them and she soon confirmed the sex of our snake. It was a small male and I knew just how he felt.

Now we had actually caught a snake, I could turn my attention to filming it. While I sorted out the camera, Chris assembled a selection of water-weeds on the grass till it looked like the surface of the swamp. What I wanted was to produce something that would look like the swamp, but without the underlying water. The theory was that I would be able to film our snake looking natural without the risk of him disappearing into the depths as soon as we released him. After all we had gone to quite a bit of trouble to catch him, and I wanted to film more than just his tail disappearing.

Cradling him like a baby, we manoeuvred our snake into place among Chris' carefully prepared film set. I arranged a few tasteful wisps of water hyacinth by his head till he looked right. Maria undid the tape that was holding the sock on the snake's head, and then she gently peeled the sock off. Chris and I watched from a safe distance.

Nothing happened. The snake looked at us, and we looked at the snake. Snakes have no eyelids, but if he had had them, I'm sure he would have been blinking away in the bright sun wondering what the hell had happened. As it was, he just lay there panting and occasionally flicking his tongue out.

Gingerly I moved the camera about till I could get a clear view of his eyes between the foliage, and started filming. On cue he flicked his tongue and moved his head a little so that the viewer would know he was alive. Suddenly I loved him. I moved nearer and put a close up lens on the camera. I was getting shots of scales moving between the vegetation: an eye passing behind a leaf. I was having fun. This was exactly what we wanted, so I moved closer.

There is something about a snake with its unblinking gaze that lets it look straight into your soul. Perhaps that was why I looked up eventually. I had spent half an hour gazing through the camera lens and inching myself closer and closer to our snake. So when I did look up I was gripped by sudden panic to find that I had got so close to him that I could have reached out and touched him. More to the point, the mouth that had mesmerised and terrified me half an hour earlier was only about thirty centimetres from my hand, well within striking range. We were lying virtually head to head and he was looking straight at me. But as I looked at him lying there he slowly lost half his power to scare me. He was just an animal in among the vegetation and I felt all the fascination for him that I had felt as a boy when I found my first newt.

Despite that, I backed off a bit and looked round to see Chris and Maria grinning away. They had obviously been having a great time watching to see just how close I would get before disaster struck. From that moment on, I mentally named each snake we caught 'Disaster' to try and remind myself that they were just waiting to strike.

Before I could do any more filming, Maria announced that she thought Disaster was getting too hot sitting in the sun, and needed to be put back into the swamp. So back he went, and we followed him to go hunting for more snakes.

That afternoon became the pattern for our days. We

wallowed about looking for snakes, and when one of us found one, we would heave it out onto a dry patch to film it. On about day three, I decided to try using a special lens that I could put almost touching the snake. I could even get the tip of the lens right underneath a snake and try out shots looking up at the sky with the snake's head literally above the camera lens. That lens is about forty centimetres long, so I was relatively safe, but it was worth the slight anxiety because when the tongue flicked out it nearly licked the lens, and that really did add a certain something to the shot.

Within a few days, I became quite good at handling the snakes we caught, but I never got over that rush of adrenaline when the weeds moved. There is something so primeval about those snakes that even if I worked with them for years, I know that finding one would always give me a buzz. Only one actually managed to hit me when it struck, and the experience left me strangely elated. For a start, it didn't grab hold of me; it literally just hit me. It hit quite hard but backed off immediately. Its teeth drew blood of course, and I was left with a ring of scratches on my leg but nothing worse than that. It was a very scary moment, but it made me realise that all that performance of striking at you is just that – a performance. It obviously knew that I was too big for it to tackle, so it used its full repertoire to try to scare me. It succeeded.

I also have to admit that I never became as proficient at finding snakes as Maria, so several times I was left with a slight queasy feeling when she found a snake in a patch that

I'd already waded through. Maybe I just hadn't been lucky enough to tread on it. However I did manage to get the record. One patch of weed I stabbed with my trusty stick started heaving a vast distance from where I was. Maria was like a dog that has flushed a pheasant.

'Where is the head? How big is it? I want to see its head. I think it is Elvira. We caught her before and she is very big.'

Unfortunately ('fortunately' would be closer to my actual thoughts at the time) there were just the two of us that day, so there was no way we could catch such a giant. To Maria's great glee though, we did see the snake's head briefly before it disappeared, and it was awesome.

A few days after that meeting with Elvira, Chris and I found her again, out of the swamp this time, and basking. It must have been the same one as we were in roughly the same place and there weren't likely to be two such giants in the same pond. To measure her we used the accepted method, which involves lobbing things (we chose flowers) till you land one near to the head and another by the tail. Then when Elvira had moved off we paced out the distance between the two flowers. You are allowed to add twenty percent to make up for the fact that a snake rarely lies straight out. That basking monster was well over six metres long with a head bigger than a Rottweiler's.

It just had to be the mythical Elvira, and I reckoned that when she opened her mouth to strike, the ring of teeth that flew at me had roughly the diameter of a football. The blithe confidence I had developed after being hit by a snake evaporated. Elvira would have been quite capable of tackling an animal my size. Her girth was about the same as my waist, and when we told Maria, she estimated that a snake that big probably weighed about one hundred and fifty kilos. And that is roughly twice my weight.

To begin with, Elvira just lay in the sun and ignored us. She didn't even flinch when we threw flowers at her, so I set to work filming her. Pictures of very big snakes were a major part of what we were after with the anacondas, so finding her that second time was a boon. But, even with a giant like her, it is surprisingly difficult to give a good impression of an animal's size on film. What I needed was something to give scale to a shot of her head, and there was precious little around that could do that. I kept moving about trying one angle after another, till eventually I managed to frame her head dwarfing a water hyacinth flower. I set the camera running and bless her, she chose that moment to slither over the flower and flatten it into the swamp. I silently thanked her. I was just lining up another shot when Elvira decided to bury herself into the mud. By now we were getting a bit blasé.

'Let's pull her out again,' said Chris.

So we both grabbed her tail and pulled. We might have been pulling a train. With no indication that she was even aware of our efforts she went on burrowing into the swamp, pulling us along with her. In hindsight that was probably the best outcome we could have hoped for. It would have taken six or seven people to catch Elvira, and if she had turned on the two of us, all we could have hoped to do was run away.

Elvira was magnificent, but the principal thing we were after was the mating of these giants. I had read that at about the end of March, female anacondas come into breeding condition. They produce a scent to attract a mate, and that scent is so potent that besotted males, lead by the nose, go looking for females. Sex-mad male anacondas trying to find the source of this perfume are liable to turn up all over the place. The swimming pool at the ranch headquarters is apparently their favourite spot, but they often get into houses and regularly get squashed on the road in their quest for a mate.

When a male finds a female he coils around her trying to mate, but that is not the whole story. As a general rule in the animal kingdom, it is the females that select a mate, and they use all kinds of ways to choose the best partner. Birds, for instance, may look for flying skill, a well-made nest or success at finding food. Large mammals may look for a particularly fine display, physical strength or fighting ability. Anacondas seem to look for stamina or perhaps persistence, because the female doesn't just mate with the first male that comes along in response to her aroma. She waits, and keeps on pumping out her irresistible perfume, so inevitably more and more males are attracted. They all wrap around the female and around each other producing the ultimate nightmare for anybody with a phobia of snakes – a mating bundle. There may be seven or eight big snakes in a bundle, all coiled together writhing in the mud, and amazingly enough, they can stay together for up to a month. Then, it's probably the one that holds on longest that gets the girl. Our ultimate ambition was to film a mating bundle.

So we spent many days wallowing in the mud, prodding the slime and watching for the telltale heaving of the weeds. We found lots of snakes, and learned that Maria's encouraging words were true. There were hardly any leeches, even fewer piranhas, and every caiman we met erupted in an explosion of mud as it dashed away. But we saw nothing like a mating bundle. We knew that male snakes were moving around, because we kept finding them on dry land. It was obviously the right season, but we had no luck.

After nearly three weeks of searching the swamps, our time was fast running out, so we held a council of war. I interrogated Maria. Are we looking in the right place? Could anybody else help us? What are our chances of finding a mating bundle? And so on. Her answers (Yes, No and Poor) were not encouraging. The mating bundle was a vital part of the programme, so along came the inevitable question.

'Is there any way we could fake it?'

Next day we abandoned our search for a mating bundle, and went in pursuit of a big empty oil drum instead. That was rather easier and we found one behind a shed, cleaned it and put it in Chris' shower. Then we collected some snakes; one fairly large female plus eight assorted males, and put them into the barrel. Animals like snakes are generally unaffected by brief periods of captivity, so their well-being was not a big worry. With a couple of rocks on the lid there was no way they could get out of the barrel, but Chris still complained about his room-mates. I suppose he had a point; the barrel rocked gently all the time and produced occasional hisses, not to mention the incessant rasping of snake scales sliding over each other.

The next day had to be our last for filming the snakes, so the moment of truth had arrived. At this stage everybody on the ranch was allowed a small bet on whether our ruse would work, and the odds ended up at around 2:1 against. The consensus was that our entire collection would head off for the four points of the compass as soon as the lid came off.

We decided to try in the cool of the morning when the snakes would be a bit dozy. We selected an attractive site, set up the camera, rolled out the barrel and opened our oversize can of worms. Out flumped a giant's portion of animated spaghetti. Snake heads looked out from every part of the bundle and snaky bodies slithered in every direction.

Beside me, Maria was jumping up and down saying that it looked exactly like the real thing. That was just as well as I had already started filming. Through the viewfinder it looked tremendous: I had a screen full of snake. I managed to get the camera almost touching them, and they took absolutely no notice of me. I had shots of snake eyes, snake heads, snake bodies and they were all slowly slithering about. All kinds of snaky things could have been happening in the middle of that heap. It looked great, and quite sinister enough to put our viewers off their TV dinner, which is always my ambition. And the betting optimists won on points because for precious minutes our bundle remained intact.

When eventually our stars all slid off, they left us in a state of elation, but for me it was tinged with disappointment. The producer and editor were going to be able to tell their story using the material we had shot, so they would be happy. I was the one who felt cheated. I had developed a respect for these vast terrifying reptiles that verged on affection, and somehow I felt that I was selling them short by filming a bogus bundle. That's the trouble with cheating: I always seem to end up feeling that I have cheated myself.

CHAPTER THREE

The Polar Bears' Picnic

As I stepped outside the hut I realised that, almost for the first time, I was living out one detail of my childhood dream. I was carrying a rifle. That was the only bit of dream that I did match, and even that was rather less romantic than it might have been because the barrel of my rifle was adorned with a toilet roll. That said, I wasn't about to leave the hut without a rifle. In my fantasies the rifle had always been protection for me and my faithful assistant in case a rogue buffalo charged us, but here I was carrying it to protect myself from an even greater threat.

I took a careful look around to check that I was alone, but it looked clear so I dropped my pants and sat myself down to use the bucket as quickly as possible. Like most people I usually sit and contemplate, but I make an exception when it is in the open air, there is snow falling, the temperature is around twenty below zero and there is a very real threat from polar bears. I was back inside the hut within a minute, and did my contemplating in the warm.

I lay down on my bed and thought about those polar bears. I had been up to the Arctic a couple of times before to film them, and they invoke very strong, but mixed feelings in me. For a start, a polar bear is the only animal I have met that looks at you the way a gourmet examines an oyster. I am sure they weigh you up judging your blubber content, and if you are lucky, they decide to walk away. But if they leave you alone, it's only because you are not worth bothering with: they are not in the least frightened of humans. They are aggressively solitary and eat seal blubber, but only about one hunt in fifty results in a kill, so they must be hungry for most of the time. They are huge, especially the males, in fact the very first bear to come and visit us in our little hut left paw prints so big that I could fit both my boots into one of them. They are one of the very few animals that may attack a human unprovoked, and I am frightened of them.

On the other hand, they are the most achingly beautiful animals I know. They move with a power and grace that is hard to match, and I have nothing but respect for any animal that can survive in the Arctic. They remind me of Wagner's Flying Dutchman because they wander the ocean endlessly. It is a magical moment when you see one appear from behind an ice flow. When you see it disappear again into the mist, you know that you have seen the most truly wild animal in the world.

I had plenty of time for these rather romantic musings because I spent ages in that little hut. Here I was trying to film bears again, and we (that is Jason, an Australian assistant and myself) had been flown to a lonely little cabin on a remote island in the Svalbard archipelago. I had worked with Jason the year before, and had real respect for him. He had lived in Svalbard for several years and had had a glorious range of jobs in his time. These included working on the futures market in Sydney, leading snowmobile tours in Svalbard, as well as the inevitable bar work that all young Australians seem to use as a world passport. He had also started the Svalbard wind-surfing club, and boasted that it had six members. He was a useful man to have around, but even he took bears seriously.

A lonely little wooden cabin beside the sea might sound idyllic, but it was hardly that. The sea was frozen. Huge nails had been driven through the window frames leaving the glass surrounded by ugly sharp spikes. The door was reinforced with great beams of wood, and all this in an effort to stop bears getting in. The general effect was of a prison cell, but one designed to keep the vandals *out*. The sobering thing was that these defences were more symbolic than effective, because if a bear decides to go into a cabin, it goes. If I was in any doubt about this, I just had to look at the splintered remains of an earlier cabin that stood behind our new home.

Virtually the first thing we did when the helicopter left

us was to surround our cabin with a military style fence. It was equipped with booby traps set to explode when the fence was touched. The booby traps were tiny explosives designed to wake us up and warn us of approaching danger rather than do any harm to an interloper, so with the fence in place, we felt relatively safe. That feeling proved to be pure self-deception when we found those huge footprints right outside our door the first morning we were there. Obviously our monstrous visitor had had military training and knew all about booby traps. He must have either stepped carefully over our fence or limboed under it, and I wouldn't put either possibility past a bear.

There were obviously bears around, so next day we started trying to film them. In front of our cabin was the twisted and tortured ice that made up the frozen ocean, and that was the direction our visitor had come from: behind us the land was covered in snow, except for the stark black cliffs that protected the island plateau. It was so bleak and barren that it made real the Vikings' idea of hell. In summer the cliffs would echo to the calls of nesting birds, but we had arrived much too early for anything as gentle as that, so it was still eerily quiet except for the vacant howl of the wind.

I knew that most of the bears, like our giant visitor, would be wandering out on the ice looking for seal breathing holes, trying to kill something to eat. But we weren't there to film those wandering bears, we were after the ones that had spent the worst of the winter in snowy dens. Only the mated females build dens, and they do it by finding secluded snowdrifts and just digging a hole. This happens in November when the Arctic is dark for twenty-four hours a day, so, to the best of my knowledge, nobody has ever seen it happen.

Cocooned in her den the female gives birth to her two cubs, and then she suckles them for about four months. The temperature inside the den probably hovers just below freezing so the young family is spared the worst of the Arctic winter, but needless to say there is nothing for the mother to eat, which means that she lives off her fat reserves. The result is the world's most drastic weight reduction regime. A female polar bear loses about half her body weight in five months, and that can mean shedding over two hundred kilos. By late March she feels that she can face the world again, so she and her babies emerge from her den. That was what we wanted to film. 'Mother bear plus babies emerging and playing around the den' is what it said on the script, and we had to put pictures to go with those fine words.

We were there at about the right time: it was mid-March and the peak time for bears to emerge from their dens should be mid- to late March. The first sunrise for months had broken the winter night sometime during February, and by the time we arrived, it was light for about eight hours a day. That was bad enough, but it was complicated by the fact that every day was nearly half an hour longer than the one before, which threw my internal body clock right out of kilter. While we were there, temperatures once climbed as high as minus five, and these are the conditions in which polar bears choose to leave their dens. What could they have done to deserve this?

We were planning to concentrate our efforts on one small valley up on the plateau above our cabin because in previous years researchers had found several dens up there. So when the sun came out on our second day there, we went to check out the little valley. Clear days tend to be cold days in the Arctic so it took us some time to get ready. First we had to struggle into layer upon layer of clothes till we looked like a pair of Michelin men. Then it was time to clip on crampons, find the ice axes that we needed to cut our way up the gully to the plateau, and shoulder the rifle we had in case a bear attacked us. It took us about an hour and a half of step cutting and climbing to reach the plateau, so we arrived tired and sweaty.

What confronted us was something like an amphitheatre, a shallow saucer cut out of the plateau. We were looking at a perfect example of what the Welsh call a 'coomb' and the Scots refer to as a 'corrie'. As a teacher in Wales, I had shown coombs to innumerable students, and tried to get them to imagine them being formed by the action of ice gouging into the rock. Here I was faced with exactly what I had tried to get those students to imagine and it was bleak. The whole valley was white with just a few of the rocks at the back of the coomb showing, so as we surveyed it, we scanned every snowdrift in case it held a den. We walked all around our little patch and finally stopped at a particularly good vantage point by a snowdrift where we could sit out of the wind, enjoy a little picnic of coffee, chocolate and biscuits while we tried to work out where there might be a polar bear den. Our coomb was not an encouraging sight.

The producer had told me back in England that she wanted me to film the bear family from the moment the mother crawled out of the den leading her two cubs. The chances of filming this were not quite as bad as they sound because once she has dug an exit from her den, the mother spends a few days perusing the cold desert that is her true home before actually climbing out. Also, after the cubs' first appearance, their mother gives them a couple of weeks to play around the den, to grow stronger and learn about the white world they will live in. During this brief playtime the family still uses the den for shelter, so they pop in and out quite often. However, after the two weeks of play, they all set off to the sea ice for a lifetime of wandering. So we were looking for tracks in the snow or a snowdrift with a polar bear's head sticking out of it.

For three weeks we searched for a den. Every day we checked the weather, and if the cloud had lifted and the blizzard had abated, we struggled into our warm clothes and climbed up to our little valley. We trudged around checking out the local snowdrifts, and each day we had our little picnic in the same relatively protected spot. After three fruitless weeks of searching we began to doubt that there were any bears in our valley at all. Everywhere we looked there were snowdrifts, but none of them sported a bear's head. One drift looked much like the next to me, so I started to wonder why we should expect our little valley to be a polar bear maternity wing. The researchers had told us that three bears had their dens there last year. But that was last year, I told myself. They also assured us that the bears should start to break out of their dens in mid-March. It was now early April. In short, I started to lose faith. Those little nagging doubts whispering in my ear had taken to using megaphones. We had no way of searching farther afield so frankly it seemed hopeless. Weather permitting, we kept on struggling up the hill and searching, but it all felt more like a ritual than a purposeful search.

Then one day we spotted a bear's head and everything changed. There it was sticking out of a snowdrift like a glove puppet on top of a duvet. To our eyes of course, it was a wonderful sight, except for one thing. It was sticking out of our snowdrift. The blood drained to my feet as the implications of this dawned on me. No wonder we hadn't found the den, we had been picnicking right on top of it. We had spent three weeks sitting on top of a bear.

Like us, she had obviously decided that in a wilderness of snow and rock, that particular drift was the most sheltered spot. With her supreme sense of smell, the mother bear must have been only too well aware of us sitting above her head. Even if she didn't fancy the smell of us (and I could hardly blame her there), the chocolate must have been irresistible. I suspect that after being shut up alone with two cubs for four months, the mother might have been just a little bit tetchy. After being on a starvation diet for five months she might have been a tiny bit peckish, and after devoting so much effort to her offspring she might have felt slightly protective towards them. It was scary even thinking about how close we had been to an extremely dangerous bear. The other thought that crossed my mind was that maybe she was late breaking out of her den because she had been waiting for the tourists to leave.

We backed off to consider the situation and for about half an hour we sat and watched our bear while she watched us. She was beautiful, but my thoughts kept drifting off to large quantities of blood, missing limbs and pain. I suspect that she saw us as a minor irritant. Eventually the stand-off ended when she ducked back into her den. I could never say that she blinked first: my guess is that she decided we were insignificant.

Once she had gone, it was time to work out how we were going to film our bears. I selected a spot for us to base ourselves, down the slope and up the other side, so that we were roughly sixty metres away from the den and on a level with it. But having sat and watched our bear for half an hour, it was obvious to me that there was no way we could just set up the camera and film. If we were to survive sitting still for any length of time in those conditions, we had to be out of the wind. We also wanted to make ourselves as inconspicuous as possible, so we set about digging a relatively spacious First World War trench in a snowdrift. It was while we were digging that it dawned on me that we had been told there should be two or three dens in this little valley. We had managed to pick the spot for one den so perhaps. . . .

Jason and I dug in turns while the other stood guard with the rifle. We gained a bit of courage from the rifle but we both knew it was little more than a gesture. If our spade had hit a bear, the first we would have known about it would have been a murderous white fury exploding out of the snow, and if that happened, no amount of weaponry would save us. Fortunately our fears proved groundless and our trench proved to be ours alone. By that evening we were all set. We had found a den, and we had sorted out a camera position, so we were ready for action. We had a celebratory feast when we got back to the cabin, and for the first time since we arrived, I believed that it was going to work. I tried to tell myself that I had never really doubted the research.

Next morning hardly bothered to dawn. Instead it hid itself in dense mist and threw snow at us with a vicious wind. The next few days tormented us with slight variations on the blizzard theme till frustration gnawed at us and we both became seriously short-tempered. Then a day came when we could at least see the cliffs behind the cabin, and we thought we might have a chance. We trudged off through the fresh snow, cut ourselves new steps up the gully, cleared out our trench and set up to film our bears. The weather was poor, but we clung to the hope that it would clear, so we sat and waited.

After about three hours the mother bear emerged, and our excitement rose till we even forgot to be cold. She was careful and suspicious, sniffing the air for danger, and watching us to see if we were a threat. She eased herself out of the hole and stood by the entrance to the den pawing the snow and examined everything around her. After a while there was a movement behind her. We tried to keep still and avoid alarming them, because the cubs were hiding behind their mother's vast body. Slowly we all relaxed, and the cubs came fully into view blinking in the light of day. They were the sweetest things I have ever seen. As their confidence grew they all began to shuffle about and soon the cubs were playing. They started a play fight. They fell into the den entrance only to climb out again. They chased each other and rolled around in the snow. They were just as entrancing as I had hoped.

We had spent four weeks waiting for just this, but now it was happening I couldn't film it. It was tantalising. We could see the bears and what they were doing was perfect. But down the viewfinder, through mist and falling snow they were grey shapes in a grey landscape. On film you would have hardly been able to make them out, and producers don't hire me to shoot useless film. I was impotently furious. I silently cursed the bears, the weather, Jason, the snow and life in general. Why was this happening to me? What was I doing here? What had I done to deserve this?

Thoroughly dejected, I sat there and tried to enjoy watching a rare and wonderful sight, but that didn't work. I tried to console myself with the thought that by watching our bears I was learning something about their behaviour so that I would be able to film them better when eventually conditions improved. With animals as hard to observe as those bears, you rarely have the luxury of a dry run and have to start filming the moment you see them. I tried to see the advantages of our situation, but chiefly I just sat there fuming in the icy cold. Eventually the light faded, the bears climbed into their den, the weather worsened and we slithered down the hill back to our cabin.

For the whole of the next week, alternating fog and blizzard kept us in the cabin. I had read my way through almost the whole of the little library I had with me, and my tapes were becoming dreadfully over-familiar. Even Mozart can seem trite with constant repetition: eight pieces of music would never be enough to keep you sane on a desert island. There was nothing we could do but wait. We knew the potential of our bears; we had seen it, but we couldn't film it. It was intensely frustrating, and it was only made worse by the knowledge that the bears would be happily frolicking around their den. A bit of mist and snow wouldn't worry them, but we were stuck.

When eventually the skies cleared, we trudged back up to the plateau, cutting new steps yet again, only to find that there were fresh bear tracks in the snow we were cutting into. An adult and two cubs had come down the gully that morning. With very little hope, we went on up to the coomb where we sat and watched the den on the off chance that it had been some other bears that had left the tracks. But nothing appeared. They must have waited for the first clear day and left. It was a very low point, and we had no real hope of salvaging anything from the mess. Jason and I sat in resentful stubborn silence watching a hole in the snow.

We repeated our unsuccessful vigil on a couple more days and if anything became more dejected. Then one evening as we were packing up, Jason suddenly had a bright idea.

'Let's have a look inside the den,' he said.

I was desperate enough to think it was a good idea so we walked over to our old picnic site. As we reached the den, my nerve started to fail me.

'We are sure it's empty aren't we?' I whinged.

We had been watching it all that day and for several days before that and nothing had stirred, so Jason didn't even bother to reply. He handed me the rifle and got down on his knees beside the hole. It was his idea, so I was quite happy to let him go first while I clutched the rifle like a toddler with a comfort blanket.

Slowly he wriggled his way into the hole in the snow, till all I could see were his crampons. Then they were gone, and I could just hear muffled exclamations of surprise coming from the hole, but he seemed to be on his own in there.

After a while, a beaming smile appeared at my feet. Slowly the rest of Jason emerged, and he climbed out onto the snow. I ran a quick check for missing limbs like a mother with a new baby till I realised he was intact and decided it was safe to copy him. So I knelt down, put my head into the hole and started downwards.

A bear, even a female after her winter crash diet, weighs at least three times as much as me, so I expected the den to have a decent size entrance hole, but it was a tight fit. Feeling like Winnie-the-Pooh I squeezed my way down for about a vertical metre till I tumbled into the den proper. What I found was no more than a horizontal tunnel about a metre in diameter, stretching two metres either side of the entrance hole. The walls were covered with deep scratches from the mother's claws, and there was a yellow hue to the ice on the floor. There is one thing to be said for living in a deep freeze though; the smell was nothing like as bad as I had expected. Actually I thought it was quite snug in there, and quickly realised that I must be going mad. I squeezed out again, and we set off down the hill.

Back in our cabin, it dawned on me that we weren't much better off than the bear family. Jason and I were sharing a hut that I measured at just less than three metres square. Fortunately we didn't lose any of our precious space to the film gear because I kept it all in flight cases, and stacked them in the wood shed at the back of the hut. The last thing I wanted was for any of my delicate equipment to warm up by being brought into the cabin. If that happened everything would be covered in condensation as soon as it went outside again, and that is a far greater risk than the cold.

We didn't expect many visitors, so our hut boasted just two chairs and a table. There were two narrow beds, a cooker, a stove, food stores and spare clothes. Looming over everything there were always clothes drying on a line strung diagonally from corner to corner. We had to take it in turns to do anything as dynamic as getting dressed. How the mother bear could live in her den for five months was a mystery. We were starting to get heartily sick of our hut, each other and ourselves after five weeks, but perhaps that was because we still had absolutely nothing to show for our efforts.

We were also running out of time. The helicopter was due to pick us up in a couple of days, and frankly I could hardly wait to get away, even if it meant having to tell the producer that we had failed to get the film she wanted. Life in our little cabin had become tense.

The next day, the wind went round to the north, the sky cleared and the temperature dropped to about thirty degrees below. We struggled into even more clothes than usual, and set off yet again up the hill to our valley. It was a toss up whether we would follow the old route to our picnic site and on to survey the whole valley, or sit and watch from the relative comfort of our trench. The trench just won, on the grounds that we would be out of the wind and would avoid disturbing any bears that happened to be about.

So there we sat wrapped up in layer upon layer of clothes topped off with a sleeping bag. About once an hour we would make some coffee and share some chocolate, but the coffee inevitably led to the greatest problem of working in these conditions. How long can you hang on till you have to get rid of the coffee you have drunk? I was reminded of a Russian saying I once heard, 'A man does not stay warm for long by pissing in his boots.'

We had evolved a 'bathroom' area behind our trench, and used it regularly. Our time was measured in coffee breaks and trips to relieve ourselves. Between these peaks of excitement very little happened. I could see nothing except rocks, snow and ice. Nothing moved so there was nothing to distract me. At least half of my conscious mind was devoted to my twin goals of keeping warm and telling myself that I did not need to empty my bladder. These two rather limited ambitions kept me occupied for hours on end as I examined one snowdrift after another through my binoculars.

If the coffee breaks were the high points, the trips to relieve myself were the pits. First I had to unzip the sleeping bag and struggle out of it. All that precious warmth – gone in an instant. Then I had to climb out of the trench and avoid slipping on the polished ice of the short path to the area of yellow snow. It was there that the full horror struck. I had to stand and strip away my many comforting layers of clothes and lose the lovely warmth that had taken two hours to accumulate. And then I had to rummage around trying to find something that the cold had withered to little more than the size of a shrivelled acorn. The loss of self-esteem was almost as hard to bear as the loss of heat. Those trips were bad enough, but my mind turned to worse possibilities. I prayed for constipation and thanked heaven for having been born male.

I was settling down after my third trip when Jason silently pointed to the old deserted den that we had climbed out of just eighteen hours earlier. Through the binoculars there seemed to be a black nose sticking out of the hole. I knew there couldn't be any such thing, but that was what it looked like. Slowly a big white head followed the nose. A bear looked straight at us and snapped her teeth in an unmistakable gesture of threat. I was horrified. Jason and I looked at each other as understanding slowly hit us.

It wasn't only the fact that we had recently crawled out of that den. We had also been on the point of walking over there when we had reached the valley that morning. After all, it was our picnic site and we had squatters' rights. We would have casually sat ourselves down beside the hole. We would have had no reason to worry, after all we knew the den was empty, we had been inside it just a few hours earlier. And then what? Cold as I was, a new chill managed to run down my spine.

For what seemed like an age we watched the bear and she watched us. When eventually she pulled her head down into her den again, we tried to forget what might have been, and concentrate instead on our new situation. While our bear was out of sight, we set up the camera, prepared spare magazines of film and cleaned lenses, all the while trying to keep quiet. For the first time in weeks the weather was perfect. It was still bitingly cold, but it didn't seem to matter any more.

Less than an hour after we first saw her, our new bear emerged fully from the den followed by her two cubs. The sun was shining, the sky was blue and the wind had dropped. The cubs tobogganed down the slope only to run up it again. One chased the other into the den, but within seconds they both reappeared. One pounced on the other while mum lay in the snow sunbathing and watching her offspring. They climbed up her legs and fell off her back. She suckled them and they fell asleep on her huge chest. They did all their tricks, and I managed to shoot about an hour of film. As dusk fell, the mother bear led her two cubs away from the den down the hill. We knew when they reached the cabin because they set off the booby traps on our fence: the mother obviously believed in starting military training for her cubs at the first opportunity. From there she must have taken them off to sea to embark on their lives roaming the pack ice and hunting seals. The polar bears' picnic was over. We had done one afternoon of filming after six weeks of frustration, but we had what we wanted. It was a moment of supreme elation.

The next day we packed everything up and skied over the sea ice to the weather station about fifteen kilometres away. There we found Oysten Wiig, who knows as much about bears as anyone in the world. It was his research that told us that there should be bears in our coomb, so he had become my hero. Excitedly we told him of our bears and the way that a second one had moved house to the abandoned den.

'Oh yes,' he said. 'They quite often move to a new den. That's why you have to be very careful before you go into a den you think is empty.'

CHAPTER FOUR

It's Just Not Cricket

IT HAS TO BE ADMITTED THAT THE immigration officers at Dallas Fort Worth international airport do not have a huge reputation for their sense of humour. They may be very efficient at detecting communists, criminals and terrorists, but as stand-up comics, they hardly score. So it was quite an achievement when we managed to get one of them to crack first a smile, and then a joke.

'What is the purpose of your visit?'

'We are here to film wildlife.'

'What wildlife you here to film?'

'Crickets.'

That is when the smile came. And the joke. 'We play baseball here. Not your English cricket.' Desperate to keep on the right side of him, I hardly registered the smile and spluttered on.

'No, no, not the game of cricket. The little insects that make a noise at night.'

By now he was having a great time with us. 'I hate those little critters. They keep me awake. Why do you want to come here to film bugs?'

I decided it was time for a backhanded compliment. 'Because we want to film them mating, and here in Texas you have the horniest crickets in the world.'

That did it. He was a large man, and he produced a genuine belly laugh. The effect was much like tap-dancing in the reading room of the British Museum. Everybody turned to see what was wrong. Had somebody written on his landing card that his purpose in coming to the United States was to assassinate the president? Everybody seemed to be looking at us expecting us to be arrested and whisked away. But to general disappointment, our immigration officer leaned over and told his colleague in the next little booth about these mad limeys and their game of horny cricket. The mirth spread and half the immigration officers could be seen to be smiling. Fortunately, they must have decided that although we were obviously mad, we were probably relatively harmless, so the officer stamped our visas, and let us into the United States of America.

I was glad he had been satisfied with a summary of what we were hoping to film, because the full saga would have taken a bit of telling. The story starts with an observation by a researcher at the University of Texas named Bill Cade.

He noticed that there seemed to be two types of male cricket. Some males do what the immigration officer had talked about; they sing all night. The others are silent. Bill then discovered that the singers get almost all the girls. Female crickets are attracted by the call of a singing male, and go towards him. The non-singing males get lucky occasionally, and they have a strategy to help them. A non-singing male hangs around near to a singing male, and waits for a female to come along. He then produces a tiny bit of song rather quietly, and tries to lure the female away from the male who attracted her in the first place. Very sneaky those non-singing males, but they still don't get the girl as often as the songsters do.

Bill's research addressed the question of why there are non-singers. Natural Selection says that they should die out rather quickly if they mate less frequently than the singers, but they showed no sign of becoming extinct.

The next thing Bill found was that the two types of male had different life expectancies. The singers had a short life but a happy one, with plenty of sex but an early death, whereas the strong silent types lived for much longer, just mating occasionally along the way. It all seemed horribly Calvinistic to me, and I was afraid that somebody might extrapolate from these little insects to humans. Fortunately, Bill discovered that it was not the hand of some avenging angel that was killing the loose-living singers in their prime, there was a good ecological explanation.

It turns out that it's not only female crickets and immigration officers that respond to singing crickets. Bill found a species of fly that nobody knew much about, and worked out that it was a major player in the drama of the crickets. The flies he found are a bit bigger than ordinary house-flies, and unlike most flies, they only appear at night. In fact, they look and behave slightly like African Tsetse flies because the female does not lay eggs: she keeps her eggs inside her body till they hatch, and then she deposits a maggot on her luckless victim. And the hosts for this parasitic Texan Tsetse fly turn out to be crickets. The female beams in on the cricket's song, and deposits her offspring on the singing male cricket. The maggot eats its way into the cricket's body, and lives inside it, progressively eating away at its host's insides. When it reaches full size, the maggot eats its way out of the cricket again to pupate. That moment signals the death of the carefree cricket that had sung all night, and the birth of a new generation of flies to terrorise singing crickets.

This was the tale we were in Texas to tell, and Bill had come back to his old research haunts to help us. Very rapidly we found that there was no shortage of crickets. They were everywhere, and we set ourselves up to film them. This involved establishing what I like to refer to as a 'Studio' in the lab that Bill used as a graduate student at the University of Texas.

Although the lab offered all the facilities we could ask for, we still had to call on a fair proportion of the 'portable studio kit' that I take with me on most film trips. This incorporates a bizarre combination of items that would surely have raised the eyebrows of our immigration officer if he had decided to examine that particular case. He would have been confronted by a collection of nuts and bolts, odd pieces of string, paintbrushes and plasticine. If he had delved deeper he would have found a strange combination of tools like a glasscutter, several clamps, specially bent bits of wire, the remains of my university dissecting kit and a large array of adhesives that I can use to stick almost anything to almost anything else. I firmly believe I could break out of most jails with my set-building kit, which is probably just as well because in half the countries I have taken it to, it would have been quite enough to get me locked up in the first place.

It only took us a few hours to construct a set for the crickets, and within a couple of days we had some excellent film of them. Then we turned our attention to the flies that were the co-stars of the show, so for a start Bill taught us how to catch flies. First make a recording of a singing cricket. Then take a portable tape recorder and attach a big cardboard cone to the front of the loudspeaker. Go out at night to a suitable spot and play the cricket call through the portable tape recorder. Examine the cone for flies every few minutes. By the end of the first week we had caught one fly. It died before we could film it.

This called for serious fly catching, so we made up several tape recorders with cones on their speakers, and spent nights wandering about hoping that flies would come to the call of our recorded crickets. We interrogated Bill to discover the best places to go fly hunting, and progressively he revealed his favourite locations. Eventually he sent us off to what he claimed was a really hot spot, and we wandered around making cricket noises, checking the loudspeaker cone occasionally. Unusually, Bill stayed at home that evening, and we soon discovered why. A police patrol car arrived with lights flashing. We got the full treatment: the night-stick, chewing gum, the lot.

'Hands on the hood. Spread your legs.'

'What you guys doing here?'

That took some explaining. Maybe it was our accents, maybe it was just that our story was so far-fetched that only a harmless idiot could invent it, but slowly the cop came round to believing us.

'OK. But go look for your flies someplace the other side of campus. I don't want you hanging around outside the women's dormitory again.' Thanks Bill.

A few days later the weather turned a bit warmer, and we caught four more flies, so we set to work filming them attacking our singing crickets. We cut a piece of turf and brought it into the lab we were using as a studio. We bought a small aquarium, put it upside down on the turf, and put a singing cricket into it. The cricket stopped singing. We waited till a cricket started singing, and put the aquarium over it. It stopped singing. We tried a group of crickets: one of them is bound to start singing I reasoned. All the crickets moved to the edge of the tank, and only started singing when they were in a corner where I couldn't film them. We just kept on trying to get crickets singing inside the aquarium, and when eventually one broke down and sang in the right place, I carefully introduced a fly into the enclosure. The fly sat on the glass or buzzed about like a fly in an aquarium.

We wasted hours like this. The hours stretched into days and then into nights (they were nocturnal animals we were trying to film), and we were running out of time. Trying to control two insects at the same time was proving impossible, as it usually does. We had totally failed to film the story in a way that was even close to real with the animals behaving relatively naturally, so we had to set about doing some serious cheating.

As an experiment, we tried mounting our little tank on top of a piece of turf, and standing the turf on top of the loudspeaker. This way we could play cricket calls at high volume through the turf. The theory was that the calls would bring the fly down from the glass, so at least we could get a shot of it on the turf. It worked and we had a shot of a fly on the grass. When we turned off the cricket call, the fly took off, so now we had the first two shots of our sequence.

'Here is a parasitic fly, that is trying to find a cricket,' our commentary would say over a tight shot of a fly on the grass. Cut to a wider shot of the fly and dub the noise of a calling cricket onto the sound track just before the fly takes off. The voice continues with the words '...and when it hears one calling, it flies off to investigate.' Good.

With only two days of our trip left we had exactly two shots of the fly: we seemed to be heading for a rather short sequence. We were getting desperate, so we decided to extend our tricks using recorded cricket calls. And in the process we moved further away from real spontaneous behaviour than I have ever done before or since, but there was no choice.

The next shot we needed was quite a wide one of a cricket with a fly on its back. Obviously the cricket had to be moving about so that the viewer could be sure what it was, so we needed a happy healthy cricket. But the fly would be very small in the shot, so we put a dead fly on the back of a live cricket. At first the cricket's movements unseated its jockey, but with the application of a drop of superglue, we had that shot.

Now there was no holding us. We needed to have a close look at the fly on top of the cricket, so a tight shot was called for. But this had to be a live fly, so superglue was out of the question. After a great deal of trial and error we eventually came up with the answer. The key was the observation that the fly would sit anywhere that cricket calls emanated from. So we took a dead cricket, put it on some grass, and fed a thin glass funnel up through the grass so that the tip was just inside the thorax of the cricket. By putting a small loudspeaker into the other end of the funnel, we could make the sound come out of our dead cricket. Radio Cricket was on the air. Lo and behold, we had our shot of a fly investigating a cricket.

What we needed now was the fly taking off from the cricket's back. That should have been easy: all we had to do was turn off the cricket call. The trouble was that by now all of our flies had either escaped or killed themselves by flying into our lights. We definitely needed the shot, but we had run out of both time and flies. So we had to improvise, and that meant using a dead fly. There was just one small problem: How do you make a dead fly take off? Answer: Get the camera in close to the fly, and position a small tube just out of the shot. Start the camera running and gently blow down the other end of the tube. The fly takes off. Obviously this meant that the cricket had to be stationary, so it was back to our dead cricket.

To sum up. We had one shot with a live cricket and a dead fly. We also had a shot with a dead cricket and a live fly. Now, just for symmetry, we added a final shot of a dead cricket and a dead fly. The shot we never got was of a live cricket and a live fly.

The amazing thing is that it worked. Cut together, these shots told Bill Cade's story. It was quite the most extravagant bit of cheating I was ever involved in, and I claim that it was only necessary because we were trying to film behaviour that was hard enough to see, let alone film. When it was all edited, Bill confirmed that it looked dead right and he's about the only person who has ever watched this behaviour, so I'm happy to take his word for it. It was the perfect paradox. Cheating was the only way we could tell the truth. But try explaining that to an immigration officer.

CHAPTER FIVE

Catch a Caiman by its Tail

MARIA WAS ONE OF THE BEST people I have ever worked with: she was certainly the prettiest. To begin with, she acted as our petite, fearless and mongoose-like authority on anacondas, and it was while we were up to our thighs in slime looking for snakes, that we learned about the research she had done on caimans, the South American alligator. So when we switched to filming them, she kept right on helping us.

We had met plenty of caimans while looking for anacondas in the swamps, but Maria had assured Chris, my assistant, and myself that when this happened, the marsh would explode in a fury of water, and the caiman would thrash through the swamp away from us. I was amazed that this was exactly what happened, but when it came to filming them, we needed rather more than rear ends heading for the horizon. Fortunately, caimans were very common in the open water, which was just as well as we needed lots of film of them.

The story we were trying to tell was about the animals' reaction to the ponds drying up during the dry season. The water level in these marshes changes by about three metres from the wet to the dry season, so the effects are dramatic. When we were there, it was nearly the end of the dry season, so the ponds were getting smaller by the day, and this produced huge concentrations of animals in the remaining open water. Some ponds held squadrons of wading birds solemnly marching across the mud spearing fish. Deeper ponds were occupied by ducks that dived incessantly to feed on the bottom. One large pond had more than its fair share of caimans, so we decided to concentrate our efforts there.

For a start we put a hide near the edge of the water so that I could film the basking caimans. Setting up the hide only took a matter of minutes, but caused enough disturbance to clear all the caimans living there from the banks of the pond so hundreds of pairs of eyes watched us from the safety of the water.

When we had finished, Chris and Maria drove off and I crawled into the hide with the camera to wait. Soon, caimans the far side of the pond were crawling out onto the bank to bask in the sun. Gradually some of the animals closer to me hauled out of the muddy water and from then on it was like watching the tide come in, as a wave of emerging caimans rolled towards me along the bank.

Quite quickly I started getting the shots I needed. A caiman crawling out of the water. Basking caimans. A tighter shot of the head as a basking animal slowly opened its mouth. A foot. An eye. A few teeth. They were getting very close. Then a big one, he must have been three metres long, lumbered out of the water, and I could swear he was no more than an arm's length from the front of my hide. I decided not to check my estimate, but felt that it would be a good idea to open the flap at the back of the hide just in case I had to beat a hasty retreat. I was thrilled to find that my big caiman's bigger brother was sunning himself right outside my back door.

Suppressing my panic, I turned my thoughts back to what I knew about caimans.

'They eat fish,' Maria had said which confirmed what I knew already.

'They don't hurt people,' she had added as we were setting up the hide. I had read that too, but found it harder to believe as I looked at my giant neighbour.

'Often,' added Chris just loud enough for me to hear.

'These guys are the cuddly little pussy-cats of the crocodile world,' was how Chris had summarised Maria's comments. But the manic grin on his face told me how much he was enjoying my discomfort.

He would have had even more fun if he had seen me an hour later inside the hide. That was when I decided I would be more comfortable if I had a bit more distance between me and these harmless, loveable creatures with their huge jaws and sharp teeth. I felt I would be able to concentrate better with them further away. Fortunately Maria had spoken the truth and my visitors turned tail as soon as I started lobbing pebbles at them.

As they left, I decided that I had all the close-up shots I needed of adult caimans. The next thing I wanted was caimans eating, and that meant fish. It meant we were going to have to abandon straightforward honest filming in favour of a bit of discreet cheating, and as it turned out we ran almost the full gamut of deception.

'How can we get some fish Maria?'

'We catch them.' Simple. So we borrowed three lines, and persuaded the cook to let us have a scraggy bit of meat for bait.

'What are we going to catch?' I asked.

'Piranha of course,' came the reply. 'They are so easy to catch and the caimans love them.' Being loved by a caiman seemed rather a mixed blessing.

So we went down to the river, where we each took a line and put a small cube of meat on the hook. Whole books are written about fishing techniques, with chapters on catching different fish, but Maria's advice on catching piranha was succinct. 'Throw the hook in the water. When you feel a fish – pull.'

So I threw my baited hook out into the water, and almost immediately I could feel a fish twitching the line, so I pulled. A clean hook emerged from the water.

'You must pull very fast,' was Maria's only comment as she reeled in the first of her many piranhas.

Chris and I just kept on feeding those piranhas while Maria kept on pulling them out. Eventually an extra slow suicidal fish managed to impale itself on my hook, and I had caught my first piranha. It was a fine fish, or so I thought. It must have weighed about five hundred grams and it had a bright red belly. But such things were incidental: it was the teeth that had to be seen to be believed. They were bare and sticking out of the front of the mouth, white, shining and sharp. The sharpness came home to me when my fish nipped me as I removed the hook from its mouth. Blood flowed copiously and I could see how they had managed to slice cubes of very tough old meat off my hook in no time at all. I decided to restrict my swimming to the pool at the ranch headquarters.

We took our catch to the caiman pool, and there we had a real treat in store. First I got Chris to throw a fish into the water so that I could see if the caimans reacted to it. React to it? His tentatively tossed fish caused an eruption. Half a dozen caimans appeared from nowhere and snapped at the fish as it hit the water. One swallowed it and the others kept snapping at each other. I was filming away like a mad thing, and very exciting it looked, so Chris threw in a few more fish for good measure, and soon I had plenty of film of caimans swallowing fish, and generally exhibiting their bad table manners. It was time to try something else.

I had noticed that as the pools dried up, the animals living in them suffered a range of different fates. The caimans can move to deeper ponds, but the fish are stranded, and dead or dying fish were a common sight around pools that were shrinking rapidly. All the big wading birds, the herons, storks, egrets and ibis gorge themselves on these fish, and the caimans joined in these banquets as well. So I thought we might try imitating that scenario.

I took a fish and put it by the water's edge of our caiman pool, just to see what would happen. By the time I sat down a couple of metres back from the water, a caiman was eyeing my fish, and very soon he emerged from the water and took it by delicately twisting his head and snout sideways. This looked like fun: I just had to work out how to film it. I didn't really fancy sitting right next to the piranha as the caiman came and took it, but that was exactly where I needed to have the camera if I was to get the most dramatic shot possible.

For a start I rigged a remote control cable to the camera. Then I wrapped the camera in plastic and put it on the ground about thirty centimetres from the water's edge. I positioned the fish right in front of the lens so that the water was just lapping around it. When everything was set I retreated and sat down with the switch in my hand to wait for some caimans to appear. Within about thirty seconds two or three of them had circled the fish, watching it, the camera and me.

Slowly the biggest one inched towards the fish, and I turned on the camera. He reached the shallow water, and lifted himself onto his front legs to walk slowly towards his meal. Then he turned his great head sideways, and delicately picked up the reward for his courage. He tossed the fish back into his huge jaws, swallowed it and subsided into the water. By my reckoning, when I came to look at the film, that caiman's jaws would just about fill the screen as he took his fish. I loved caimans. We tried again, with much the same result, but it is always worth having several takes of a really good shot. Then we tried the same shot at a different spot on the bank, another one looking along the edge of the water rather than out into the pond, one looking down on the fish as the caiman took it, and just about every variant we could think of. Just as we were running out of ideas, I decided that having a really big group of caimans around the fish would be fun. So I tried attracting animals by showing them the fish, and walking along the edge of the pond drawing them to the spot where I had the camera. We kept on trying different versions of the shot till we had run out of fish, and I decided that we had probably got enough film of adult caimans eating fish.

I was very excited about the shots we had just got, but as we were packing up, I noticed that Chris had become rather quiet. Eventually he started talking about what we had been doing. 'I think we got a bit carried away there. They may be little pussy-cats that only eat fish, but they have big teeth. Their brains are only about the size of a matchbox you know, so they might easily have gone for the fish you were carrying rather than wait for you to put it down. You'd never have been able to keep them or anything else in focus with only one hand.' Maria agreed, and I felt rather chastened.

Our story about caimans and the ways in which they respond to the drying out of their habitat was coming along nicely, but as usual we needed more. Then one day we were lucky enough to spot a whole gang of fifty or so baby caimans solemnly plodding across dry land.

'Their pool has dried up. They must find a new pool,' said Maria. 'I see them like this often at this time of year.' They fitted our story perfectly, so we set to work filming them.

'But where is mama?' asked Maria. 'Mama should stay with her babies.' I had heard about the way that female caimans, like most crocodiles, protect their young by keeping them together in a crèche. I had also heard that when the mothers are looking after their babies, even caimans become aggressive.

Fortunately for us, there was no mother with this lot, so filming them was relatively simple. However, I wanted dramatic shots of them making their epic journey across the drying land. Cracked mud, dry grass and the searing sun, these were the backgrounds that would tell the story, so I got Chris and Maria to organise the little creatures for me. That was how we learned that baby caimans have very sharp teeth. They were about thirty or forty centimetres long and they could move fast, so you needed to be pretty quick to grab one by the tail before it could turn round and bite. By the time we finished we all had bleeding fingers, but we also had film of baby caimans marching across country, through tussocks of grass, down slopes and finally across the cracking mud into a fresh pond. Their odyssey was complete but I still needed the shots that would start the sequence. I needed to film a group of baby caimans leaving their almost dry pool.

So we cast around looking for a group of baby caimans in a small pond. Luck smiled on us and we found just what we needed. Maria commented that it was a bit of a mystery that there was no mother with these babies either, but we just accepted that it was our lucky day and I set up the camera at the edge of the water. I dispatched Chris and Maria to the far side of the pond so that they could wade into the water and gently nudge the babies out towards me. On my word Chris and Maria slowly squelched into the muddy water and the baby caimans started swimming in my direction.

One or two of the babies climbed out onto the mud so I was avidly filming them when Chris shouted out, 'It's quite deep in the middle. How much farther d'you want us to go?'

'Little bit more if you can,' I sang back.

I finished a close shot of a baby at the water's edge, and looked up just in time to see Maria's mystery explained. A large caiman surfaced in the middle of the pond and began snapping fiercely at Chris and Maria. I tried but failed to swing the camera round fast enough to film the confrontation but Chris and Maria were on the bank before I had even focused. When we realised that there was no damage done, we all fell about in relieved laughter. The trouble was that we still hadn't got our shot.

'No problem,' said Maria. 'We catch the mama. Then the babies will do what we want, so we chase the babies out of the pond. When you finish, we put them back, and let mama go.'

'How do we catch mama?' asked Chris and I simultaneously.

'Oh, I catch caimans all the time for my research,' said Maria.

'How?' asked Chris and I again in chorus.

'I show you,' said Maria brightly. So we watched as she took one of our swamp stabbing sticks and attached a thin piece of cord to it. The result looked like a primitive fishing rod with a noose instead of bait.

'Watch. I get the rope over her head. Then I pull my end of the rope, and we catch her.'

'Yes, but then we have a very angry caiman on the end of a rope. How can we do anything with her.'

'Easy. You see.' This woman was unreal.

So Maria waded into the pond with her crazy fishing rod. The caiman snapped at her a few times, but her heart wasn't in it. Slowly, Maria reached out with her stick and neatly slipped the noose over the caiman's nose. The first few times the animal moved at the critical moment, but after a while Maria succeeded. Carefully she manoeuvred the noose back along the animal's head, past the eyes till it was behind the angle of the jaw. All this time the caiman was just watching Maria, and paid no attention to the rope that was progressively encircling it. It was as though it was trying to prove Chris' point that caimans really aren't very bright.

Finally Maria decided that the moment had come, so she pulled on her end of the rope. It tightened around the caiman, and she had indeed caught it. A fine battle ensued with Maria at one end of the rope and the caiman at the other. With most women Maria's size it would have been an unequal match, and even with Maria it was quite a contest.

'Help me,' shouted Maria. So I grabbed hold of Maria's end of the rope and together we pulled the caiman out of the pool. That animal was about two and a half metres long and must have weighed something like fifty kilos, but like most reptiles, caimans have relatively poor stamina, so her struggle with Maria and me was soon over. We put her (the caiman – not Maria) in the shade of our Land Rover, tied her to the bumper and put a sack over her head. There she lay, quiet and settled.

After all the excitement, we went back to filming the baby caimans leaving the drying up pool. That produced a few more bleeding fingers, but nothing more significant than that, and we managed to get the shots I was after. But then we had a problem. How do you release a caiman once you have captured it?

'I hold the head.' This of course came from Maria. 'James, you do this.' She showed me how I was to sit astride the back end of our caiman, holding the hind legs and tail.

'Chris, you take the rope off her head. I hold her mouth shut.' Chris duly removed the rope as Maria held the jaws shut.

'Now. Chris you go away.' Chris went off to watch proceedings from a safe distance.

'I count. *Un, Dos, Tres,* and we jump away.' I was trying to learn Spanish while I was in Venezuela and, with Maria's help I had already mastered numbers up to ten.

'Are you ready, James?'

'OK,' I said with a hint of uncertainty in my voice. I

wanted to tell Maria that this might not be the best moment for my next Spanish lesson, but wasn't quite sure how to say so tactfully.

Maria, Chris and I never quite agreed about exactly what happened next. Maria maintains that she called out loud and clear, '*Un. Dos. Tres.*' And then she jumped clear.

Chris agreed with Maria.

What I heard was something like 'Undotre,' and at about the same moment, I saw Maria jump away.

What we all agreed about was that once she was clear of the caiman, Maria joined Chris watching the animal from a safe distance. What they saw was me, and I was sitting astride a caiman's hips holding her tail. What I noticed was that nobody seemed to be holding her head. I think she realised what was going on at about the same moment because her head whipped round and lots of teeth tried to take a large chunk out of my right knee. Having me sitting on her tail must have put her off her stroke a bit, because she missed, not by much, but enough. She whipped round the other way and had a go at my left knee.

What we had forgotten of course was that our caiman had been lying in the shade for about half an hour, and had got her breath back after the excitement of being caught. So she was fresh, rested and ready to deal with her tormentor. That was me. I could tell that she didn't like what was happening, but I wasn't too keen on it either. She began to thrash wildly from side to side, left, right, left, right till she got into a regular rhythm. Her back legs were pumping away at the same time, and I could see that she was slipping forward between my legs. This was giving her increasing freedom of movement, so each snap came closer than the one before. Her teeth looked quite big when all this started: now they were enormous, and her gape was growing till I was convinced she could take my whole leg off with her next snap.

It seemed to go on for ages, but it was probably only seconds till I managed to work out her timing. I waited till she was heading for my left knee and jumped off right. I was free, but decidedly shaken.

Once we had parted company, she gave a few more snaps in my general direction, and rushed back to her pool, where her babies gathered round her. We humans just looked at each other in a state of shock. I got my breath back and decided I was feeling a bit sick, so I sat down for a while. I also decided that in terms of pushing caimans about to film them, we had probably gone about as far as we could. More to the point, we had completed our sequence.

CHAPTER SIX

Protective Custody

THE DAY AFTER I LANDED IN Australia, I found myself aboard a beautiful catamaran sailing along the West Coast to a tiny bit of fly-dirt on the map, with the name 'Salutation Island' written next to it. We were there to meet and film an extremely rare native Australian: unfortunately it was a rat, and a nocturnal rat at that. It was not just any old nocturnal rat though; it was the Greater Stick Nest rat. One of the things I love about Australians is the way they make no bones about things. They call a spade a bloody shovel, and a big rat that makes a nest of sticks is a Greater Stick Nest rat.

On Salutation Island it was hard to see what all the Stick Nest rat fuss was about. The island was littered with piles of sticks. The whole place was clearly over-run with Stick

Nest rats. There were sticks, nests and rats everywhere. The important thing about Salutation Island though is the fact that, apart from a couple of zoos, there is only one other place where you can see these animals at all, and that is another tiny island, this time off the coast of South Australia.

The story goes that in 1994 there were less than a hundred Stick Nest rats in the world and about twenty of them were introduced to each of these two islands. The island groups thrived, so there must be at least three thousand now, and the species has been saved from extinction – for the time being. There is even the glimmer of a worry that the populations on the two islands may be getting above a sustainable level. There is also the worry that with all those sticks around, one lightning strike and the whole of Salutation Island would go up in flames, wiping out half the world's population of the rats.

It was hard to remember that these were incredibly rare animals when I was surrounded by them on the island. But their brush with extinction was central to the story we were here to tell, so we settled down to film them. They are totally nocturnal, and filming them involved generators, cables and lights before we even started with the film gear. But by dusk we got everything set up and shortly after dark, even with the lights on, out came the rats.

If ever an animal needed a PR consultant, it is the Greater Stick Nest rat. They are delightful little creatures that could do with a new name. They are about the same size as ordinary rats but they have short friendly noses rather than the mean pointy ones of proper rats. The result is that they look a bit like giant gerbils, and gerbils are very popular pets. Stick Nest rats have much bigger eyes and none of the creepy sneaky behaviour that reinforces everybody's hatred of true rats. I try to tell myself that I hate rats because they are a health hazard or because they are one of the greatest non-human ecological disasters, but the truth is that I simply hate them. Fortunately, Stick Nest rats are nothing like their ordinary namesakes, so I decided we should abbreviate their name. I tried out a whole series of abbreviations that seemed to me to have an appropriately Australian flavour, but 'stickies' had other connotations and 'nesties' didn't really work either, so eventually I settled on the acronym SNR, and we agreed to call them that.

SNR nests are big, sometimes as much as a metre high, and spreading over a good two or three square metres. Each nest is home to a small group of about half a dozen animals, and they defend their territory aggressively. I am not sure about the composition of those groups, and there seems to have been remarkably little research done on the species, but my guess is that they are family groups. They feed chiefly on seeds and insects, but they loved the peanut butter that Tim, my excellent assistant on this trip, had thought to bring along.

This was the first time I had worked with Tim, but he had worked with another cameraman for many years so he had a good understanding of what is involved in filming animals. For many years he has also been a falconer and has the rare type of patience that is needed both for his sport and for manipulating animals for filming. This was to prove vital in Australia because so many of the animals we filmed there were captive and needed careful handling. However, the SNRs were the first things we filmed, and they turned out to be some of the easiest animals on our list.

I watched my chosen family of SNRs slowly emerge from their nest, and the night's activities started with a great deal of yawning, a bit of Tai Chi followed by a gentle wander around their territory. Then it was down to business and some serious looking for food, which involved a lot of digging, climbing the bushes and checking out the farther reaches of the territory. This was when the SNRs' problem revealed itself. They are totally unafraid of people – or anything else for that matter. From my point of view it was wonderful of course: all I had to do was sit still for a little time and they came right up to me. Getting them hand tame would have taken no more than a few minutes but you could see that this mindless courage could be a problem with other visitors. Strategically positioned lumps of peanut butter quickly had animals in the best-lit, most picturesque spots, so filming them was a joy. After two nights we had all the film we needed, so we sailed back to base.

Base for Tim and me was on Peron Peninsula, a huge finger of land that sticks out of the West Coast of Australia into the Indian Ocean. Here we spent our time filming several other native Australians that are on the verge of extinction. As if being wiped out wasn't bad enough, their plight is made even more poignant by the fact that hardly anybody has ever heard of them. We filmed sweet strange creatures with names like mala, bilby and fat-tailed dunnart, but it was tricky because they were all in elaborate cages or enclosures.

These creatures are all extremely rare marsupials that have only ever lived in Australia. A mala is a sort of wallaby with large, vulnerable, beseeching eyes and sensitive mobile ears. A bilby is a burrowing creature about the size of a domestic cat that conservationists are trying to promote as the Australian replacement for the Easter Bunny. The idea is that rabbits are such a pest in Australia that people's warm feelings towards bunnies are not helping wildlife, whereas bilbies are native Australian animals that need all the warm feelings they can get. A dunnart is a manic creature a little bigger than a mouse but more like a shrew in behaviour because it is a fierce little carnivore that eats things like locusts and even the big venomous spiders of the desert. Like the SNRs, all three of these species are just about hanging on in protective custody because it is too dangerous for them to live on the remainder of the Peron Peninsula. That's not as strange as it sounds because living wild anywhere else in Australia would be pretty hazardous for them too.

The hope is that in a few years it will be possible to release SNRs on the Peron Peninsula. Then it should also be safe to release the collected bilbies, mala and so on that we had had to film in their enclosures. The habitat is perfect for them and most of the peninsula is a nature reserve so they should do well. There are just a couple of small problems that have to be sorted out first.

Work has already started on these problems, and we spent a day filming one of the rangers on the project. Together we drove to the base of the peninsula till we bumped into a fence so we turned left and drove alongside the fence.

'I drive the fence every day checking for damage,' Bill told us.

I wanted film of him at work, telling us all what he was doing, so Tim had wired him up with a microphone, and I squashed myself into the passenger seat of the Land Cruiser so that I could point my camera at him as he drove. That way I managed to film him talking, and I could have the fence he was talking about in the background as we bounced along. Unfortunately there was no room for Tim in the car, so he ended up rattling around in the open back trying to work the tape-recorder while keeping the dust out of it.

'That fence is four metres high, topped with electric wires,' Bill went on. 'D'ya see there, it goes about a hundred metres out into the sea. It does that at both ends so nothing can get through it or round it.'

We reached the one gap in the fence, where the road that joins the peninsula to the mainland cuts through it. Bill got out, and we filmed him as he checked the equipment at the gap.

'We've got a huge cattle grid here,' Bill went on, 'and you see those posts, they're some kind of electronic gizmos. See what happens when I walk up to them.'

The whole place looked like a high-security prison, so I

would hardly have been surprised if he had set off a barrage of sirens, spotlights and automatic machine guns. But no. A recorded dog barked out of Bill's electronic gizmos. It sounded like a big dog, but it was still a bit of an anti-climax.

'It doesn't seem like much,' said Bill answering my unvoiced reservations, 'but it keeps the bloody things out.'

I loved it because Bill had expressed the point of our film so neatly. These impressive fortifications were not there to keep animals on the Peron Peninsula, or to keep people out of it. The fence was there to keep animals away: two very ordinary animals, the European fox and the domestic cat.

'And it works,' Bill went on. 'Look here. All around the gap in the fence we've cleared the vegetation from the sand and covered it with oil. Any footprints on there and I'd know a fox had got through the fence. Never had one get through yet. Old Bonzo there does the business.' Bill patted one of the posts affectionately, 'He sees them off.'

Cats and foxes are very familiar animals, and they sound relatively harmless, but they are public enemies numbers one and two for conservationists in Western Australia. Both species were introduced to the continent, and between them they have hunted at least twenty native mammals to extinction. It was thanks to them that Tim and I had to film all those animals in captivity, and they are the lucky ones that have been saved from extinction.

Foxes were brought to Australia deliberately so that the English ex-patriots would have something to hunt as a distraction from governing the colony. Fox hunting never controlled fox numbers in Australia, or anywhere else for that matter, so they thrived, and have easily outlasted the English government officials.

Nobody is quite sure how cats reached Australia, but there were certainly none there until Europeans arrived. They probably came as domestic pets, or perhaps as sailors' cats that jumped ship after a very long sea voyage.

Once in Australia, both foxes and cats spread, and this is where the ridiculously trusting behaviour I had enjoyed from the SNRs comes in. The small native mammals in the Australian desert had no natural predators, so they have never evolved fear of other animals. Like the more famous Dodo, they just wander up to things and investigate them. At one moment when I was filming a mala, I sneezed and alarmed it. In its panic it hopped about one metre away and froze. It was laughable, but that was its panic reaction. You could just see a fox licking its lips and smirking. One metre is perfect pouncing distance. The cats and foxes must have thought they had landed in some sort of catty or foxy heaven. Meals come to them. The native animals are food that hops conveniently onto a plate: the whole of Australia is their supermarket, and they have taken full advantage of it.

The idea is that the whole of the Peron Peninsula should be a cat- and fox-free zone. The fence is a vital start because it cuts the peninsula off from the rest of Australia, and turns the whole area into a virtual island, and a large island at that: Fortress Peron is over a hundred thousand

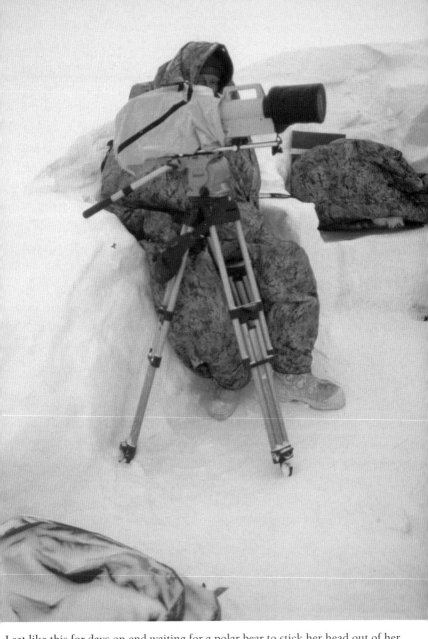

I sat like this for days on end waiting for a polar bear to stick her head out of her den. It was twenty degrees below zero so I was wearing about seven layers of clothes topped off with a sleeping bag. (*photo James Gray*)

ABOVE I love polar bears because they have absolutely no respect for humans. They usually left us alone, but I think that was because we weren't worth eating. (*photo Philip Lovel*)

Polar bears are such a danger on Svalbard that you should never leave your hut without a rifle even to use the toilet bucket. (*photo James Gray*)

In an effort to give my shots real impact, I managed to get my camera (and myself) touching this anaconda. I felt relatively safe because the snake had just eaten a meal and it wasn't in the least interested in me. (*photo Chris Barker*)

These Canadian garter snakes were just a few of the twelve thousand that I filmed in a small pit in Manitoba (*photo James Gray*)

Maria and this medium sized male anaconda probably weighed about the same, and it was all she could do to hold it back from the camera so that I could film its head. (*photo Chris Barker*)

The common blue damselfly was the star of the first wildlife film I sold. It took me four years to make the film, and this was one of the trickiest shots to get – the female laying her eggs underwater. (*photo James Gray*)

Maria seemed totally fearless when it came to handling reptiles. These baby caimans were hardly dangerous, but their teeth were like needles. (*photo Chris Barker*)

Caimans are said to be the gentlest of crocodiles, but when it came to filming them as they took fish from right in front of the lens, I decided not to sit with my eye to the view-finder. The cable allowed me to control the camera from a relatively safe distance. (*photo James Gray*)

In the dry season the river Orinoco virtually stops flowing, and we found huge concentrations of water birds gorging themselves on stranded fish in the remaining pools. (*photo James Gray*)

Each of these hairy sausages was a 'set' made to resemble a piece of my scalp. I made them out of dirty plasticine and my own hair so that I could film lice. (*photo James Gray*)

BELOW It might seem like cheating, but by filming this Australian thorny devil in a set I have a far better chance of seeing it behave naturally than if I tried to film it in the wild. (*photo Tim Borrill*)

ABOVE The central desert of Australia should be home to dozens of strange native mammals like this bilby. Unfortunately we had to film most of them in captivity because they have become extinct in the wild. (*photo Tim Borrill*)

The feral cats that infest the Australian desert have hunted dozens of native animals to extinction. (*photo Tim Borrill*) hectares – larger than the Isle of Wight. The trouble is that there were foxes and cats inside the fortress when the fence went up, so Bill's colleagues are trying to get rid of the enemy within.

We had no chance of filming people trying to get rid of foxes for the happy reason that the foxes have all gone. The rangers used a poison known as 1080, mixed it with dry feed that foxes love, and dropped the baited food pellets from a plane. All we could film were notices warning dog owners to keep their pets on a lead because there are still baited pellets lying around.

1080 was originally synthesised during the Second World War as a weapon, and a very nasty weapon it would have proved if it had ever been used in anger. Then, after the war, botanists found to general amazement that the same chemical occurred naturally in several plant species of the genus Gastrolobium in Western Australia. Zoologists then worked out that the native animals have evolved toler-ance to 1080, but foxes come from areas where the poison doesn't occur naturally, so have no such immunity. That discovery made it possible to propose 1080 as a specific poison to kill foxes without damaging the native wildlife in Western Australia. The theory was that the native animals could eat it without ill effect: foxes would eat it and die. And that is exactly what happened; there are no more foxes on the Peron Peninsula, and large areas of the mainland desert have also been cleared of foxes.

Unfortunately, cats are much smarter than the average fox, and they just will not take bait. As a member of a cat owning family, I can confirm what a picky eater our Charlie is. All cats are, and it's one of the things that have made them so successful. If the tinned cat food is more than a few hours old, Charlie turns his nose up at it. As a species they just do not scavenge, and attempts to get rid of cats by putting out bait have failed. So Tim and I went out with a ranger called Bruce on cat patrol when he was checking his traps. On that one day, Bruce caught eight cats. He shot them, and I filmed him doing it.

Like most cat owners, I was horrified at the thought of killing cats. It all seems totally wrong when I've got Charlie on my lap. I know that there is an element of self-deception there because even domestic cats do terrible damage to wildlife, but those cats in Australia really are different. They may be descended from ordinary domestic cats, but they have gone wild and have lived wild for generations so now they are correctly described as feral. Over the years they have evolved so now they are larger then an average domestic cat, they are almost all tabby (the original colouring of cats) and they are killing machines that desperately need to be controlled.

'We use leg traps,' I was filming Bruce as he set out more traps, and Tim was recording sound. 'They just hold the animal, and they're pretty painless. Then I can come along in the morning and shoot them.' This really wasn't much fun, but I felt it was important for people to know what was going on.

As he worked, Bruce kept on talking, and I kept on filming him, 'Here, I'll put a trap right by this bush.'

He set the trap, scattered sand all over it, and then sprinkled cat urine and faeces on it. I was very disappointed when our editor decided he couldn't use Bruce's blunt and typically Australian description of what he was doing at that stage, but we picked up his voice again when he went on. 'They won't take bait, but a cat's very territorial, and it'll check out any cat smell it finds in its patch. So I put out some serious cat smell to bring 'em in.'

The trapping programme has killed over two thousand cats in the space of two years, but there are obviously still plenty of cats in the reserve. Until they are gone, the native mammals will have to remain in their protective custody.

After filming Bruce killing cats, we naturally had to film the feral cats themselves, and once again we had to resort to captive animals – well pets actually, which was a real irony. We had filmed the native animals in captivity because they are very rare but not shy enough. Now we wanted to film domestic cats because feral ones are too common but very shy. So we arranged to do an interview on local radio and appealed for owners of tabby cats to contact us if they wanted their pets to become film stars. Domestic tabbies look pretty much like the feral animals, so I was quite confident that we would be able to get away with filming one. The only real difference would be the size, and for once the difficulty of giving viewers an accurate impression of the size of an animal would help us rather than cause its usual headache. We had several replies, and eventually selected our star, whose name was Sophie.

Tim and I found an enclosure that might have been a

derelict tennis court, and filled it with stunted bushes so that it looked like the outback. We wanted to film the sequence at night so we pointed some whopping great lights at the set and put filters on them so that it would look like moonlight, and we were ready. That evening Sophie came along and we put her into our set.

Sophie had 'temperament' coming out of her ears. She turned up with her agent, or owner as she preferred to be known, so we sat together watching our star on set. For a full hour, Sophie would do nothing but walk around our set yowling to be taken home. Then she came and sat at our feet and refused to move. After another hour, she relaxed, wandered around and began investigating the bushes. It looked good so I started filming. What I wanted was brief shots, a glimpse of cat here, a shadow there followed by a tail twitching behind a bush, and it was just as well that was what I wanted because that was exactly what I got.

It was a great start, but as usual, we needed more. Tim made a dummy mouse and put it on the end of a piece of string. He tossed it out onto the sand and slowly pulled it back towards himself. He made it twitch, he even tried making it fly over Sophie's head. He tried everything, but Sophie was far too sophisticated for playing kittenish games. She pointedly ignored Tim's mouse till eventually he put it in a bush, and made it twitch just as Sophie came past. She heard the rustle, turned, crouched and wiggled her backside the way Charlie does when he sees a butterfly. I was filming away, and eventually she made her pounce into the bush. Killer at work. We had the vital shot.

Then we tried to get her to eat something. The story was about these ruthless killers eradicating species after species, so we needed a bit of eating to extend the pounce into a sequence. We had managed to get hold of a freshly dead mouse but Sophie just wouldn't touch it. She gave us a withering look, which said that she was way above that sort of bucolic repast. Dead mice indeed. Did we really expect a sophisticated star cat to touch that sort of offal?

Eventually we had the idea of putting some nice fresh tinned cat food into the body cavity of our dead mouse, and we tried again. That was more like it. With a patronising glance in our direction, Sophie set to and ate it, so we had our killer. Filming trained or captive animals may be the only way to get a sequence, but it is never predictable.

The story we were filming was a strong one, and Sophie was a central part of it, but the irony was that our programme was not actually about the Peron Peninsula. The subject of the programme was meant to be the arid centre of Australia, the desert with the plants and animals that live there. We had had to start fifteen hundred kilometres from there on the coast filming animals that by rights belong in the desert around Alice Springs, because their best hope of survival may well be at Peron. The feral cats have cleared the desert of so many of the animals that used to live there.

When eventually we flew to Alice Springs and started work there, we were shown a very poignant sight. At the back of a cave there was a vaguely familiar looking pile of sticks. This is where SNRs belong, and this is where they used to live, but the only ones between Alice and the sea are in a zoo. The nest I looked at has probably been empty for the last forty or fifty years, which is the length of time there have been feral cats in the area. Now there are cats all over the place, and the native SNRs have to be held captive on an island because the cats have been able to adapt to desert living, while the native animals have no defence against the introduced killers.

One of the researchers we worked with in Alice Springs had a bumper sticker on her car that gave her opinion of cats quite succinctly and, though I decided not to take one home, in the Australian context I could see her point.

It read, 'So many cats – So few recipes.'

CHAPTER SEVEN

The Great Call of The Wild

'WHEN I GROW UP, I want to be a gibbon.' I heard myself saying these words and realised that I'd come out with two truths in one throwaway line. First, I suspect that all wildlife cameramen have a serious Peter Pan complex. I may not be a thing of beauty, but certainly I'll be a boy forever. I'm less sure about camerawomen, but maybe that's why there aren't very many of them.

The second truth is that gibbons have to be my favourite animals. I first met them as a student when the head keeper gave us a tour of the primates at London Zoo. He showed us that most of his animals regarded him as one of their own kind, and responded appropriately. So Guy the gorilla rolled his eyes at him, the chimps made kissy faces, and the male gibbon went ballistic. He flew up and down his cage swinging weightless from branch to branch while singing his wonderful song. He whooped higher and higher up the scale till he reached a crescendo somewhere north of high C, at which point his partner joined in.

'That's the Great Call,' we were told. 'They sing it as a duet to defend their territory.' It made such an impression on me that for months I dreamt of seeing gibbons for real, and I spent hours in the bath imitating their call.

Twenty years later I went to Thailand and was amazed to find that the dawn chorus in the forests there is punctuated by gibbon duets and they can be heard for miles. We seemed to be surrounded by gibbons but a terrible disappointment came with the pleasure. When I tested out my much-rehearsed gibbon call, there was no response whatsoever from the real animals. Three years of study, a degree in zoology and regular practice in the bath counted for nothing when I was confronted with the real thing. But, that was a small disappointment compared with my excitement at hearing wild gibbons. But the best thing was my reason for being there: I was making a half-hour programme about gibbons.

We were based in Khao Yai, one of Thailand's National Parks, because it held a family of gibbons that had been studied for years by Warren Brockleman. He was a delightful soft-spoken American at the university in Bangkok, and he had agreed to let us film his habituated animals.

'For a start,' said Warren, 'I'll introduce you to my study group.'

Up into the forest we went, surrounded by huge trees

and exotic bird song. It was the end of the wet season, so the forest dripped constantly, the ground was slippery with mud, and there were leeches on every low branch just waiting for you to brush against them. My mind flashed back to Humphry Bogart in the film *African Queen* when he emerges from a swamp with dozens of the things clinging to his back, and I remembered shuddering at the sight of them. They were freshwater leeches of course, but now I was looking at the first land leeches I had met. Blackish things about a couple of centimetres long, they look rather like a piece cut out of a rubber band when hungry. Once one has had a good meal (and that means blood) it swells to look like a black rubbery worm that has swallowed a kidney bean. Like so many parasites, they inject an anaesthetic and an anti-coagulant as they bite, so it is painless at the time but intensely itchy afterwards, and very likely to turn septic.

'I always spray myself with insect repellent,' Warren advised. 'It keeps the goddamn things off.' That might help tomorrow, but today was the problem. Constant vigilance was the only answer, but I still managed to get bitten. Warren walked on slowly, listening and watching all the time.

'I think they're over there,' he announced after a while, pointing away across a gully. So we set off down the gully and up the next hill. And the next gully and the next hill, till suddenly in the tops of the trees above us there were gibbons. I was in some rapturous seventh heaven to be near the animals I had fantasised about for so long, and a dozen leeches took advantage of my moment of joy to get a good meal.

There were five animals in the troupe, and Warren introduced them all to us. There were Mum and Dad, plus two adolescents and a baby.

'When I started studying this family,' Warren was telling us, 'the male there had a different wife. She died, I guess, and it took him a while to find a new partner. But since then they've had these three kids plus one other, a male, who left home some time back.' I seemed to be listening to the synopsis of some soap opera, but I knew that it had taken Warren nearly a year to habituate these animals, and he and his students had studied them since then. As a result, most of the research into the behaviour of wild gibbons has been carried out on this troupe.

'They're a fairly typical family group, and their families are pretty much like human ones,' Warren explained. 'The parents only have a baby every two or three years, and the young ones stick with their parents till they're five or six years old. So that one there, the older son, must be just about ready to leave home.'

'And the Great Call?' I asked. 'What chance have we got of filming them when they sing their great call?'

'That's a matter of luck,' he replied. 'Well, luck plus effort. They'll sing most mornings, but it'll be early in the morning when it's just getting light. If you're here at that time, you might get lucky, you never know.' My heart sank. I knew that Warren had skirted around another important thing about the great call that I had read up about. As far as I could make out from the literature, a couple only sings the Great Call once or twice on any particular morning. It's not like most bird song in the dawn chorus when the male starts belting it out just before sunrise and keeps it up for a couple of hours or so. We were only going to get one shot at it per day, and the odds had just slipped from bad to awful.

'That Great Call,' Warren went on, 'it's the basis of their marriage. We think it maintains their pair bond as well as their territory. It certainly tells the neighbours that the territory's occupied. It also tells everybody around that ma and pa are alive and well, and that they're still united. It means that there's no point in trying to annex even a part of their territory.'

What I needed to work out was how we were going to film it, but Warren had only one more bit of advice to offer us on that score.

'They're quiet now, of course,' he went on, 'but it's quite late in the morning. They spend the morning eating. What you want to do is find a fig tree that's just coming into fruit. That way, you'd get all the film you want of them eating. They love those figs. You might even get them singing in any fig tree that fruits in their territory because they damn near set up camp and live there.'

He went on to tell us of trees dripping with fruit and swarming with animals eating the fruit. He told us of a complete rainbow of small birds as well as larger ones like hornbills. He held out the promise of a banquet attended by gibbons of course, but also monkeys, giant squirrels and even the very shy binturong. This last I decided was an invention of Lewis Carroll (And hast thou seen the

Binturong...) but he assured me that it was genuine, and that it looks like a cross between a shaggy cat and a squirrel. So now we had two Holy Grails for the film (if you can have two Holy Grails): the Great Call and the Fruiting Fig.

Warren's troupe was well-habituated and quite happy for us to come close to them. We could even stand directly under them, so that was how we started trying to film our gibbons. For a couple of exhausting weeks we slithered around in the mud with the camera gear, following the troupe and trying to get a decent view of them through the leaves. Every time the animals moved I had to move, and that was quite a performance. First I would skate around in the mud till I could find a spot that gave me a view of our stars on their new branch. Then we had to take the camera off the tripod, shift everything to the new filming position and put everything back together. Only then was I ready to start filming again, but the moves often took so much time that the gibbons had shifted again before we were set up. I spent far more time moving and setting up the camera than filming which made it incredibly hard work.

The trick with the insect spray worked well at keeping leeches off, and just to prove it, Jane-Marie, who was my assistant on the job, carried out an unintended experiment on it. One day she sprayed only one of her boots and by midday when we sat down by a river to have our lunch, she had blood oozing out of the unsprayed boot. The leeches had obviously managed to crawl into her boot through the lace holes, but by the time they had gorged themselves on her blood, they were so fat they couldn't crawl out again.

The anti-coagulant they inject means that the wounds they make carry on bleeding for hours, hence the blood seeping out of Jane-Marie's boot. We took twenty-seven well-fed leeches off her foot. The only revenge we could come up with was to throw the leeches into the water and watch a shoal of little fish eat them.

We battled with the rain, mud and leeches for a couple of weeks, but then the wet season ended and the glorious dry season started. The rain stopped, the mud dried up and the leeches disappeared so we all heaved a sigh of relief. The following week the tick season started and they were at least as disgusting as the leeches. They weren't particularly good at crawling through lace holes, but if you looked carefully you could see ticks sitting at the tips of twigs or leaves waving their little hooked forelegs waiting for you to brush against them. As soon as one caught hold of you it started to crawl upwards, and only stopped when it had reached a dead end. 'Dead end' in this case meant your waistband, your crutch, your armpit, your nose, your ear or your hatband, and at the end of every day we all spent half an hour or so inspecting ourselves and each other in a hunt for feeding ticks. A lighted cigarette or smothering the animal with vaseline usually made a feeding tick haul its mouthparts out of your skin, but we all ended up with quite a collection of suppurating bites.

I only mention these parasites to stop people thinking that the job was undiluted fun. At the same time, I mustn't give the impression that it was all misery either, and despite the drawbacks working with those gibbons easily lived up to my hopes. For one thing we were getting some good shots, but above all we were filming real wild gibbons at home in their forest. The problem was that quite soon it became repetitive. With our gibbons at the top of a tree, and us at the bottom of it, they were always thirty or forty metres above our heads and our view of them wasn't very flattering. Their backsides aren't their best sides. We simply had to get on a level with them, so we moved on to plan B.

Plan B involved building platforms high in the canopy so that we could join the gibbons and share their perspective on the world. We'd all been on a climbing and rope course back in England, so in theory we knew exactly how to do it. In practice we stood with all our ropes, caribenas and slings at the foot of a tree gazing up. There were no low branches, no hand holds and the trunk was so vast it could have been a polished wall for all the hope we had of scaling it.

Help came in the form of Peaw, a wonderful man who lived in the park. He'd helped Warren in his work, and had built towers for the BBC to film gibbons some years earlier. He knew what we needed far better than we did, so he and his helpers constructed ladders out of saplings and attached them to the trees. Soon ladders snaked their way up likely looking tree trunks to dizzy platforms strung crazily together in the canopy. Then Peaw set up pulleys and ropes transforming the forest into an adventure playground with a series of circus high-wire platforms.

Sitting on a small platform up in the canopy of a rainforest, fifty metres above the ground was an unforgettable experience. The trees below me resembled clouds seen from a plane, their rounded billowing shapes stretched to the horizon. The colour reminded me that they weren't clouds, but the greens were so varied that they made a picture on their own. The odd streak of colour marked the path of some exotic bird or other, and occasional waving branches told me where the gibbons were.

Unfortunately, what those waving branches usually told me was that the gibbons were nowhere near my platform. That was hardly surprising because getting set up took at least forty-five minutes, and created quite a disturbance. We simply had to find another way to approach the problem. Richard Davies, the other cameraman with me, decided to cut out all the commotion of climbing the ladders and hauling up his camera gear in the early morning by spending the night on a platform. He tied himself on and said it was a great experience, but he didn't try it very often, and it was still pot luck whether the gibbons came near to his platform or not. Usually not.

It was time for Plan C. This involved Peaw and me driving all around the park looking for fruiting fig trees next to the road. The theory behind Plan C was that Warren's study group had been habituated to people by seeing them around for years and being unharmed by them. So, I thought that gibbons with a territory that included a road might be habituated to cars, and might regard them as harmless. It was a nice theory, but Plan C never produced much.

At about this stage a sound recordist named Keith

Desmond joined us. Being a bad golfer, he was fascinated to see that there was an eighteen-hole course in the middle of the park. I never discovered why it was there, and till Keith arrived I had been rather disdainful of it. Looking at it afresh I realised that it offered us great stretches of forest with large clearings frequently occupied by people waving metal sticks, talking, swearing and shouting 'Fore!' It was just possible that gibbons might be living in these stretches of forest, and that they would be blasé about people behaving strangely. So the golf course became Plan D.

We got some strange looks as we heaved our cameras around the course, but the golfers there must have been quite used to unusual hazards. Outside the clubhouse was posted a local rule: 'If your ball becomes lodged in an elephant foot-print, you may take a free drop within one club length of the spot.' It must have been a challenging course because instead of the usual long grass, the rough was fifty-metre high jungle containing interesting hazards such as tigers, clouded leopards and king cobras. There was also a Buddhist monk who had established himself in a small patch beside the thirteenth fairway. We never discovered why he lived there, but I hope he inspired passing players with the serenity that is so vital to a good golf swing.

Plan D was more productive than most of its predecessors. The chief thing that the golf course gave us was a lovely view of gibbons moving. There was one long narrow strip of forest between two fairways that the resident gibbon family used regularly as a highway to travel from one part of their territory to another. We could watch, and film them swinging from tree to tree, and I even managed to film them there in slow motion. We were making good progress, but both of our Holy Grails, the Great Call and the Fruiting Fig still totally eluded us.

This lack of real success was becoming worrying when we heard of a place in the south of the country where they had captive gibbons in a sort of zoo. I was doubtful about how much use it could be, but we formally designated it as Plan E, and went down there to have a look anyway.

What greeted us was quite a surprise. I had anticipated lots of miserable animals in tiny cages, but what we found was just a few apparently fairly normal animals in a series of large outdoor enclosures. Each enclosure consisted of a number of trees and had a boundary not of high wire as I had dreaded, but of water. Gibbons are totally arboreal creatures so they never naturally come down to the ground and there is no way they would swim a moat. As a result the gibbons were contained without us having to look at them through netting.

By sheer good luck, one enclosure held a family just like Warren's habituated group that we'd been filming in the forest. There were the mother and father accompanied by a full-grown son, an adolescent daughter and a small baby. Suddenly I could get the close-up shots that I hardly even dared to hope for. They had seemed so unattainable while I was up in the forest that I'd banished them from my mind, but here they were relatively simple.

The mother lay on a branch while her baby sat on her chest and occasionally leant forward to suckle. The father hung onto a branch with one hand, surveying the world about him, and for once I could get a close-up of just his hand and then I could tilt down his arm to find his beautifully expressive face. When the wind blew, the baby climbed up into the branches and had the time of his life being whipped about on the original white-knuckle ride. The match was perfect, so these shots of captive gibbons could be edited in with the 'natural' filming we'd already done in the forest. Footage from the one setting showed gibbons in their natural habitat, the other gave us close-ups to add impact and drama to the film.

What we still hadn't filmed was the Great Call. So every morning at the zoo we were up before dawn waiting for our gibbons to sing for us. And every morning they sang their wonderful duet, but they always managed to be on the other side of a tree or at the far end of the enclosure. Invariably they only sang once each morning. It showed us how optimistic we had been even to hope to film the Great Call in the forest. If we couldn't do it with gibbons a few metres away from us in no more than a dozen trees, what hope had we with relatively shy animals in a territory of about a square mile?

Then one morning it all just clicked. There, right in front of me, the male hung from a tree and I started to film him as he began his song. He went up the scale from tenor through counter tenor to alto and up to surpass any known treble. And when he could get no higher without stunning bats, his wife, sitting next to him, joined in with a cadenza to turn his aria into a duet.

Beside me Keith was recording the sound, and when eventually I turned the camera off, we just looked at each other. We'd done it. It was a stupendous moment. At last I felt that we were going to do justice to these wonderful animals. I was still grinning while we had breakfast. I really had no idea how the whole programme was going to go together, but I felt confident that a competent editor would be able to make a good programme out of it. As it turned out an excellent editor, called Mark Fletcher, made a prize-winning programme out of it.

A few days after we left the zoo we had to pack up and head home for Christmas. In my case this meant dispatching the camera gear, and getting into holiday mood because my wife Caroline brought our two daughters out to Thailand so that all four of us could have Christmas on the beach. I picked them up from the airport, and we went straight to a hotel near Khao Yai where I had been filming. They wanted to see what I had been doing for the last three and a bit months, and I rather enjoyed being able to show off my local knowledge though I didn't expect they would see very much in a couple of days.

The next morning I took them into the park, and we drove to a particular spot I had earmarked. I still had lingering hopes for Plan C (the trees beside the road), and I vaguely thought that one particular tree near the campsite might be coming into fruit. We drove there: it was in fruit, and it was everything that Warren had promised. I was speechless from a mixture of shock, pleasure, frustration and joy. All I had to do, in fact all I could do, was point at a tree not thirty metres from the car and my family could see the whole story I had been trying so hard to film for three months. Everything was there. The tree was dripping with fruit and swarming with animals. It held a rainbow of small birds, plus hornbills, gibbons and giant squirrels, and it was the best view I'd had of any of these animals in the three months I'd spent in Thailand.

The bad news was that my camera was on its way to London so I could only gaze at this wonderful sight and bemoan the fact that I couldn't film it. The good news was that my camera was on its way to London, so I could simply revel in the glory of what we were looking at rather than worry about how to get the best shots and whether I had missed anything. The best thing was that the whole family was there to enjoy it with me. Emma and Kate, our daughters, never could understand how I had spent all that time filming what they'd seen in one day. I had to admit that they had a point, but then, they had seen one of the most wonderful sights in nature. Mind you, there was no binturong, but I never really did believe in them.

CHAPTER EIGHT

I Counted Them All Out and I Counted Them All Back In Again

NOT FOR THE FIRST TIME, a disembodied producer's voice down the phone started things off.

'Could you do a bit of studio filming for me?' was all he said, so being an ambitious young cameraman, the answer came out automatically.

'Yes. I'd love to.'

'I'll get the animals to you by post,' he went on. 'You'll be pleased to hear that we're getting them from a research lab, so there's no possibility of infection.'

This left one or two questions hanging. 'What are these animals? What do you want me to film?'

'Oh. Didn't I tell you?' Pause. 'Human lice are what I am after.' Another pause. 'I need them egg laying.'

Great. As the parent of young children, head lice were no great novelty to me, but caring for them, nurturing them, getting them into breeding condition, all this was new. Poisoning them, squashing them and eliminating them with eye-stinging shampoo were more in my line.

He was talking again. 'I found one source that could supply them, but they would have been taken off down-and-outs arriving at a night hostel. They might not have been very savoury. The point is that if you're to get them to lay eggs, they'll have to be very well fed, and they only thrive if they are fed regularly... on human blood.'

This had to be a joke. I had worked for organisations that wanted metaphorical blood from employees, but he was going way beyond that. What would an industrial tribunal have to say about this?

I ran through all this in my head, while my jaw remained stubbornly slack and my mouth hung open. A goldfish would have been more coherent, so I let the silence hang.

'The lab ones don't carry any infection,' the cheerful voice said down the phone. 'They're really clean. And they don't even hurt when they bite. They don't itch or anything. I'll put you onto the people at the lab; they can give you all the details of how to look after the little things. What we want is film of them laying their eggs on human hair. The lab people can tell you all about how to get them to perform.' With that he was gone.

And so it was that I received a small package through the post containing forty lice and for the next couple of weeks they became my charges. They were about three millimetres long which is a bit smaller than a sesame seed, so they are easily big enough to see with the naked eye, but small enough to lose quite easily. They couldn't move particularly fast, so they were nothing like as hard to deal with as fleas would have been, but tricky none the less.

Every day I cleaned out the petri dishes that I kept them in and gave them a new piece of slightly damp paper. Morning and evening I gave them a feed, and it became a ritual. First I made a ring of Vaseline about five centimetres in diameter on the underside of my left forearm to act as a fence and stop them colonising me too thoroughly. Then with a small paintbrush I meticulously lifted my lice out of the petri dish and put them on my arm in the centre of the Vaseline circle. Taking them out I counted them obsessively, and then just watched them feed.

It took about twenty minutes for the forty pale, skinny little things to settle down and gorge themselves. To my great surprise, the producer had spoken the exact truth when he claimed that they wouldn't hurt. I could hardly feel them while they were feeding, and the bites didn't even itch afterwards. Presumably they inject a small amount of anaesthetic like the leeches in Thailand, because I really couldn't feel a thing as they bit me, but there was none of the bleeding that leech bites leave you with, so any anti-coagulant they inject must be on a much more modest scale. I imagine that lice in the 'wild' pick up all kinds of bacteria and other contaminants so that when they bite they inject a horrible cocktail of germs into you, and that must be what makes the bites itch.

I couldn't say that I made friends with my lice, but right from the start they were much less awful than I had expected. That said, anybody who is thinking of getting a pet should take my advice and look for something more loveable than lice. They really don't respond to kindness, and though I came to accept them, and even felt protective towards them I never developed a very close emotional relationship with them. We kept things on a purely physical basis. Yet I spent a lot of time with them and thought a great deal about them. These were the animals that had got deeper into the language than almost any other. 'Lousy' is one of my most frequently used insults, and it was one that my family applied to me liberally at the time. A wonderful insult I remember hearing once went, 'Only your lice will mourn you when you die.'

During one twenty-minute feeding time, my mind wandered to the way these little things on my arm had nudged the course of history. I seemed to remember from some dim and distant lesson that during the First World War they were the vectors of trench fever, which killed more people than gas, bullets or bombs. Yet here they were painlessly getting fat on my arm. That evening I decided to learn more about my charges, and discovered that they cause quite a few skin complaints and are the vectors of diseases like epidemic typhus and relapsing fever. I knew about typhus, and knew that it was a good one to avoid, and though relapsing fever sounds vaguely nineteenth century it's still probably worth missing.

I also discovered that Burns wrote a poem to a louse that

he spotted on a lady in church. I copied it out and learned it while I fed my charges.

> Ye ugle, creepin blastit wonner,
> Detested, shunned by saunt an' sinner,
> How daur ye set your fit upon her,
> Sae fine a lady.
> Gae somewhere else and seek your dinner,
> On some poor body.

I was fascinated by the elitism of wishing the parasite onto 'some poor body' rather than a 'fine lady', and I still wonder where I fit into Burns' social scheme of things.

As they drank my blood I watched my lice change from small grey commas to dark round bullet points on my arm. Then, as each one became fully gorged it would start moving around and that was the moment I was waiting for. 'One move and you're out' became the rule. With obsessive care I put them back into their petri dish. I counted them all out and I counted them all back in again.

I had chosen the underside of my arm because there are fewer hairs there than on the upper side. Lice that are well fed (and I considered mine to be exceptionally well fed) tend to go into egg-laying mode when confronted with a patch of hair, and the last thing I wanted was to have my arm covered with nits, which is what louse eggs are usually called. However, egg-laying was exactly what I did want to see: I simply had to see it down the camera lens.

There was of course no way that I could film them on an

actual bit of human hair. For a start I was a bit short of volunteers, and I could hardly put my own arm out and film it at the same time. Then there was the problem of size. Adult lice are pretty small, but their eggs are tiny, less than half a millimetre was my guess, and that's only a bit more than the width of a human hair. What I needed was the shot of an egg appearing from the back end of a female, and virtually filling the frame as she stuck it to the base of a hair. To film things that size, everything has to be rock solid, so nobody would be able to keep still enough. I had to fabricate a bit of human scalp.

First I went and had my hair cut. The local barber was a bit surprised when I asked him to sweep the floor before he set to work on me, but he was totally amazed when I started collecting what he cut off. At least it gave him something to talk about rather than asking whether I had been on holiday yet. Then I gave Kate, my younger daughter, a bit of a shock when she caught me gazing intently at my hair in the bathroom mirror.

'Did you lose one of your pets, dad?' she quipped.

'No.' I replied rather tersely. 'They are all fine. Thank you.' These family jokes were starting to wear a bit thin. 'I'm trying to see what my scalp looks like close to.'

'Well yours is full of dandruff.' Thanks Kate.

She would have been surprised to learn that she had actually given me an idea of how to emulate scalp. My thoughts had started to focus on her and her current addiction – modelling animals out of Plasticine. As any parent will tell you, white Plasticine quickly takes on a dirty greyish colour as you squeeze it about in your hands. What I was looking at in the mirror looked remarkably like well-loved, much-squeezed Plasticine. All I had to do was stick tufts of hair into the stuff and I would have scalp. I decided that adding dandruff would be taking realism into the realm of the disgusting.

From then on it was plain sailing. Each of my sets was a piece of my replica scalp, about one centimetre long and a quarter of a centimetre wide. I put a couple of lice onto each set, and arranged them so that I could watch them all and bring the camera lens to whichever louse looked the most likely to start performing.

For the first day or so they all just sat there looking rather pathetic and doing next to nothing, so I decided that they were a bit on the cold side. After all, I reasoned, they must be accustomed to living at human body temperature, and the studio was well below that. I turned up the heating and my lice became a bit more active, but they still weren't laying any eggs or even mating. Next I raised the humidity by surrounding the tiny Plasticine sets with damp tissues and spraying the whole thing regularly. That was better, they seemed to be much more comfortable, but still no sex.

Lice that refuse to breed sounds like a dream come true for people working in public health, but for me it was a problem. The only other reason I could think of to explain their abstinence was that they were hungry and weren't getting enough food to produce eggs. I was giving them a gut-full of my blood twice a day and that felt to me as though it should be enough, but it was the only thing I could think of. So I added a mid-day feed to the morning and evening meals, and that did it. The day after I upped their rations I spotted the first pair mating, and within a few hours they were all at it. I decided to film them mating, and as night follows day I soon had them egg-laying as well. I failed to film the first two or three to lay eggs, but I soon worked out exactly what they do. First a fat female would crawl down to the base of the hair. Once she reached the plasticine she would turn round, crawl a couple of millimetres up the chosen hair and stop. That was my cue, and I could start filming in the sure knowledge that she would produce an egg inside a minute. In a couple of days I had the sequence, and sent the film off to the lab for processing.

Once I had heard back from the producer that he was happy with what I had shot I knew I had succeeded. My final dilemma was what to do with my stars when I finished filming them. Normally I am meticulous about releasing animals back into their natural habitat. In this case the natural habitat was only too close at hand, but releasing my lice to colonise me seemed to be taking conservation a bit too far. The lab they had come from were adamant that my lice were now no longer clean, and they didn't want them back. That struck me as a bit rich coming from people who dealt in human parasites. I felt personally insulted but I could see their point.

Eventually I hardened my heart, stopped myself thinking of them as my charges, and reminded myself that they were human parasites, the vectors of innumerable diseases, and the definition of dirtiness. One last time I counted my forty lice as I took them out of their petri dish home. I put them with their eggs and all the Plasticine sets into a polythene bag and sprayed the whole lot with insecticide. I felt terrible about it, but only I mourned my lice when they died.

CHAPTER NINE

Little Brown Jobs

AS ANTICLIMAXES GO THIS WAS ONE of the best. I had just flown five thousand miles to Santiago in Chile, and the producer wanted me to film a boring little bird. The bird concerned was a thing called a fiu-fiu, and my mouth sagged in open disbelief as I read from the book that its name '... accurately imitates this little bird's gentle call'. I had come all this way to film a little bird whose claim to fame was a song that goes 'fiu – fiu'. But there was more to come. A fiu-fiu, I learned when I looked at the picture, looks very much like a female chaffinch, which is one of Europe's dowdiest birds. So I was here to film a brownish finch-like bird; a 'little brown job' if ever there was one. A nondescript bird with a tedious little call hardly seemed like a recipe for stardom to me, but Crispin, the producer, was adamant.

'It might look and sound boring,' he conceded, 'but its story is fascinating.'

'Let me tell you about it,' Crispin went on. He was not going to give up. 'Every spring, in November (remember we are in the Southern Hemisphere), at least forty million fiu-fiu arrive in Chile: they are summer visitors.'

'Oh come on. There are hundreds of summer visitors, and they all arrive in about November. Let's film something attractive. How about some of the humming birds. They're amazing little things. We could really do something with them.'

His reply was a little terse. 'I am glad you mentioned them, because they're part of the same story, and you'll need to film them too.' When will I learn to keep my mouth shut?

'The thing about the fiu-fiu is its migration. All the other migrants get to Chile from the North following the Pacific coast to the warm plenty of the Southern summer.' He was waxing lyrical, which is always a dangerous sign, or per- haps he was just gearing up to write the script before I had even filmed the story.

'Fiu-fiu come from the East. These little birds cross the Andes twice a year because they breed in Chile but over- winter in Brazil and Uruguay or somewhere around there. The lowest passes through that part of the Andes are about four thousand metres high, and when the birds make the journey, they have to battle deep snow and freezing temper- atures. That is the story we are going to film.'

I had to accept that it was a good story. These fiu-fiu

were obviously amazing little things, and they deserved respect, but it was still going to be quite a task to make them attractive on screen. Our conversation took a turn for the better when Crispin suddenly asked, 'Can you ski?'

I adore skiing, so next day we drove up to a ski resort near Santiago with the excuse that I was going to film the high Andes in snow. The idea was that these pictures would carry the words about plucky little fiu-fiu flying through snow-covered passes to reach the Shangri-La of Chile in spring. Suddenly I loved fiu-fiu, and their epic journey. Looking at the mountains I even came to respect any bird that could cross them. Big mountains the Andes, and a huge obstacle to a very small bird.

The filming only took a couple of hours, and for the rest of the day we were able to dump the camera and enjoy ourselves. That included getting to know William, who was to work with me for the whole of my time in Chile. He had a splendid dry sense of humour, but his most obvious quality was the fact that he spoke good Spanish: less immediately apparent was his ability to speak every other language you could think of. Mention of Russia brought a couple of minutes of unbroken Russian from William. Similarly when I told him I had worked in China, he started speaking flawless Mandarin. It was only when I happened to mention Germany that I worked out the secret behind his infinite ability as a polyglot. I speak a bit of German, but still it took me a full couple of minutes to realise that William was sprouting pure drivel with an excellent German accent. It was like listening to a gifted German two-year-old making language noises. There was a liberal sprinkling of words in there like 'Ja', 'Nein' and 'Achtung' but it made no sense at all. My eyes opened like portholes as understanding dawned, and when I started to laugh, William joined in.

'I wondered how long it would take you to rumble me,' he said.

'If you had just kept clear of German and French, you could have gone round the full United Nations,' I replied.

'I suspected that German might be a bit risky,' he went on, 'but I just had to try it.'

The truth was that he had an amazing ear for language, and could imitate the intonation and speech patterns of virtually any language he had ever heard. He did also have a real gift for language, so the Spanish was genuine, which was just as well because otherwise we would have hardly made it beyond our skiing trip.

A few weeks later we moved several hundred miles south of Santiago to an area of temperate rain forest on the island of Chiloe. We wanted to be all set up and ready to film the fiu-fiu when they arrived with the spring though this was no penance because southern Chile is spectacular. Almost anywhere you go in Chile the mountains of the Andes make a sensational backdrop to a view, and in Chiloe this is particularly true because at that point the Andes consists of a wonderful line of perfect volcanoes. One or two of those symmetrical snow-capped cones trail a wisp of smoke just to remind you that they are still active and waiting to blow, but that only makes them more magical. In front of them the forest bursts into flower in spring with an unrivalled explosion of blossom: the colour scheme is an almost perfectly co-ordinated range of reds. The red theme starts in an under-story of fuschia and continues up into the canopy with at least a dozen species of tree all flowering at once.

The flowers of this forest have evolved to meet the needs of their particular pollinators, so both the red colour and the open trumpet shaped flowers proclaim the fact that these flowers have evolved for the use of birds. Humming birds are the specialists, and the migratory ones had arrived with the first explosions of blossom, but the fiu-fiu were scheduled to join the feast very soon. I love the thought that this entire forest flushes red for the benefit of these tiny animals. The fiu-fiu story was getting better as we worked on it.

That relationship between the flowers and the birds revealed an interesting side of Emma, the Chilean researcher William had hired to help us. She had a degree in biology and had done research on several of the things we were to film – not the fiu-fiu, but other stories on our 'Wants' list. She joined William and me in our delight at the way the forest turned red, and marvelled with us at the beauty of the birds that fed on the flowers, but she balked at my comment about the co-evolution of those species. Her dilemma came from the fact that she was a fundamentalist Christian, and believed in the creation as described in the bible. She clearly suffered agonies trying to reconcile her strongly held beliefs with the ideas of evolution that underlay so much of the biology that fascinated her. Chiloe was particularly stressful for her because it is one of the places that Darwin visited on his famous voyage on the *Beagle*, and he refers in his diary to several of the animals we were working on. Emma was a lovely person to work with, and while with her I became uncharacteristically silent about my own view that the ideas of evolution show the biblical account of creation to be little more than an interesting myth or at most an allegory.

Setting to one side these eternal questions, we prepared for the arrival of the stars of our show. That involved filming the humming birds, and within hours I was regretting my blustering comments to Crispin about 'really being able to do something with them'. They were great to watch, but, when I tried to film them, I realised that they fly as fast as thought and only pause for the briefest instant to drink from a random flower before flitting off again. I had often seen humming birds and marvelled at them, but had never tried to film them before. My attempts, or rather my failures, sobered me up considerably.

I positively welcomed the fiu-fiu when they arrived because anything had to be easier to film than the humming birds. The first we knew of the fiu-fius' arrival was their plaintive little song all around us: their incessant 'fiu – fiu' sounded like applause for the spectacle of the crimson forest. The little birds had descended upon the flowering forest in their flocks, bringing Crispin's story to its climax. I could almost hear the narration describing the scene I was watching.

'After their long and arduous journey over the mountains, these tiny birds desperately need to feed up to recover their strength and prepare for the breeding season ahead. And here waiting for them are the forest's rich offerings of nectar, so they gorge themselves in this storehouse of plenty.'

I just had to get the pictures to go with the purple prose. First I selected a flowering tree that I could see fiu-fiu feeding in. Then I rigged the camera for slow motion filming, and bolted a huge telephoto lens onto the front of it. The birds seemed to feed by fluttering from flower to flower, so, for simplicity's sake, I started by trying to get the relatively wide shot. I spotted a bird, and lined up with it perched in the middle of the frame. Then I had to hope that it would fly to a flower somewhere in the shot. It was rather a modest plan, but it still proved hit and miss because it was so hard to predict where and when the bird would chose to feed.

I was getting through film at an alarming rate, and having so little success that my patronising comments about these birds and the sequence in general came back to haunt me. To make things worse, I phoned Crispin and he made it very clear that what he wanted was the extreme close-up shot of just the flower with the bird hovering and feeding. He wanted to make the point that although the fiu-fiu are not much good at hovering, it's worth the effort for the huge reward of the nectar. That was the whole point of the sequence, and he was dead right: we needed that close-up shot.

Disappointment was turning into total failure when I belatedly tried to consider the problem analytically. For a start this meant watching carefully what the birds were doing, so I abandoned the camera and just sat with my binoculars. The first thing that became clear was that describing a fiu-fiu as 'not much good at hovering' was pure flattery. I have seen bricks do better.

Then I noticed that a feeding fiu-fiu just sits on a branch for quite a bit of the time. Without warning it takes off, flies to a flower and flaps desperately for a brief moment till it falls back onto its perch. The whole exercise takes at most a matter of seconds. From the point of view of filming, the speed with which they fed presented a huge problem. From the point of view of the story we were trying to tell, it was great because the effort the birds put into getting the nectar showed how desperate they were, and how valuable the food was to them. Unlike the humming birds, fiu-fiu are not specialist nectar feeders, for the rest of the year they feed on seeds and the like, and only turn to nectar when it is in super abundant supply. But, I had to film them feeding on nectar and they looked even trickier to film than the humming birds.

As I watched, I managed to work out some more details. I decided that a fiu-fiu, surrounded by flowers, must select the individual flower it was going to feed on by sight. Through my binoculars I could watch a bird sitting on its perch, twisting its head from side to side, gazing this way and that: it just had to be looking for the best flower. But what made a flower look good to a fiu-fiu?

Pondering this problem, I made my second important observation, and soon the whole thing made sense. I noticed that the fiu-fiu did most of their feeding in the morning, so early one morning I went and had a close look at the flowers. In most of them I could see nectar glinting at the base of the petal trumpet, but occasionally I spotted one with a trumpet so full of nectar that it was literally dripping with the stuff. I reasoned that a fiu-fiu is useless at hovering, and it has a short stubby beak so it could only feed on flowers that were oozing nectar. These had to be the flowers that the fiu-fiu were looking for.

These little brown jobs were smarter than I had reckoned. They didn't waste their energy on the paltry rewards offered by most of the flowers. No, they went for the jackpot every time – for them it had to be flowers that were full of nectar or nothing. At last I had a theory to explain what was happening, so it was time to try manipulating the fiufius' world.

I should say at this stage, that filming animals by manipulating them in the wild is one of my favourite ways of working, and this is partly because it involves dipping my toe into the world of the confidence trickster. I want to make it clear right away that I am not a con man, at least not in the sense in which the police use the term, and everything I know about their world comes from that prince among films, *The Sting*. As Paul Newman's character explains, the key to a successful sting is preparation and background knowledge. Your experienced con man spends ages weighing up the situation, and above all studying the person he is going to sting, who is known as the 'mark'. Then, when everything is ready, when the con man has a full and deep understanding of what makes his mark tick, when the mark is gagging for the bait, the con manipulates just one or two things, and the trap is ready to spring.

Life seems normal to the mark, as he walks inexorably down the primrose path that the con has chosen and cleared for him. In total ignorance, he plays what he imagines is his normal role, behaves as he always does without noticing the subtle changes that the con has introduced to his world. Inexorably the mark takes the bait and in ignorance he gives the con what he wants. It is the most elegant of tricks, the most satisfying form of deceit.

In my version of the game, I was of course to play the Paul Newman role, and after a couple of days of preparation, it was time for the sting. I felt I had done my homework, and had a good understanding of my identified mark, the fiu-fiu. From what I knew of their behaviour, I decided that a honey-trap was the type of sting we should go for. In this case though, I wanted to apply the phrase literally and use honey as the bait. But before we could go ahead, I had to persuade Emma that the cheating I proposed was legitimate. Her strict morality posed a severe test of my argument, which was along the lines that we were only trying to encourage natural behaviour, so my proposed cheating was not lying. The distinction I was trying to make between cheating and lying is rather a fine one, but eventually I convinced her, and we set to work.

I mixed a teaspoonful of honey with water till it made a slightly viscous liquid. In a small ceremonial procession, we carried our bait out to the nearest flowering tree, and set

SNARL FOR THE CAMERA

about working out which flowers to doctor. Part of my background research had generated two sets of criteria for choosing a flower. On the one side there were my demands, but these had to be set against the bird's needs. I wanted a flower that was immaculate so that it would look pretty. I also wanted to film flowers that were fairly low on the tree so that the birds would be more than mere silhouettes against the sky. And of course, my flowers had to be on the sunny side of the tree so that the birds would look their best. The birds seemed to need a flower that was about forty centimetres above a suitable perch because that seemed to be the distance they usually flew to feed. The perch had to be a bare length of twig that was roughly horizontal.

Armed with a syringe-full of our artificial nectar, Emma and William set about finding flowers that met our joint requirements. We soon worked out that it was best for me to sit in my filming spot, and direct Emma and William as they did their flower doctoring. The whole performance was reminiscent of the gardeners painting flowers in *Alice in Wonderland*, and we provided a dialogue to match.

'Can you reach that flower just up and left of the one brushing your nose?'

'That one?'

'No. One further this way.'

'That's too far from the perch. How about this one? Can you see it from there?'

It went on like that for some time till eventually we had a selection of baited flowers. William sarcastically shouted 'Action' to the fiu-fiu, and he and Emma left me to my vigil.

Within half an hour a bird started investigating the area around one of our doctored flowers. I sat still and waited till it settled on the perch that we had so carefully identified. That was my signal to move, but my movement had to be measured so as not to alarm my potential star. First, I had to find the relevant doctored flower down the viewfinder, and that took a bit of time because all the flowers looked much the same. Once I was sure I had the right flower, I locked the tripod so that the camera remained exactly as I wanted it. With everything locked steady, I could focus the lens perfectly on the flower. By now, the bird was out of shot, so with my finger on the camera button, I took my eye away from the viewfinder. That way I could watch the bird and shoot in the secure knowledge that the doctored flower was perfectly in frame, ready for the bird to visit it.

The first few times, I got over-excited and switched on the camera as soon as the bird moved from its perch, but each time it went to the wrong flower and I was left wasting film and cursing. However, after a while I worked out that I could relax a bit. Once a bird found our nectar-filled flower, it would feed, settle back onto the perch and then go back and feed on the same flower again two or three times. Emma and William had taken to putting so much nectar into their flowers that a mere fiu-fiu could never drink it all at one visit: hence the return trips to exhaust this surprise bonanza. Now it was relatively easy. Spot a bird as it flew to the perch and frame up on the doctored flower. Wait for it to feed on the flower once, and then about five seconds after it had settled on its perch, turn on the camera. Almost every time the bird was back at the doctored flower within a few seconds, and I had my shot. A couple of days later I had what we needed.

The spin-off from our efforts with the fiu-fiu was that the humming birds became relatively easy to film as well. The fiu-fiu had to make several trips to empty a flower that we had filled, but a humming bird could drain the fullest flower at a sitting because they can hover for ages. By doctoring a number of flowers next to each other, we found that we could attract humming birds to our chosen flowers, and once there, a bird would spend several seconds emptying them all. As a result, I got some lovely long slow motion shots of them hovering, feeding and manoeuvring from one flower to the next.

The whole exercise was incredibly rewarding. Here were wild birds, and we had managed first to understand what they were doing, and then to manipulate them into doing it to our bidding. But the real reward was being able to watch these birds minutely. Through my huge telephoto lens all I could see was a stunning red flower, and a little bird sipping nectar from it. Only a total Philistine could fail to appreciate them.

They looked even better when, a few weeks later, we came to view the film and watch the birds slowed down six times. I already knew that humming birds are consummate masters at hovering, but to watch them in slow motion was pure joy. That way you can see how one positions itself with pin-point accuracy for its tongue to probe the tube of a flower, and then re-position itself for the neighbouring flower before streaking away.

By contrast we confirmed that a fiu-fiu can hardly hover at all. On film we could watch a bird fly up into frame aiming like a paper dart for the drop of nectar. Its trajectory had to have the flower perfectly at the zenith of its climb because it has virtually no manoeuvrability while at the flower: it had to flap desperately to hover at all. After a brief moment of sipping at the food, the bird tumbled back out of the shot again. By counting the frames I managed to work out how long a fiu-fiu spent at the flower, and the answer was about half a second. No wonder I had problems trying to film it without manipulation.

Watching them on film finally sealed my attitude towards the fiu-fiu. Even while we were working with them my opinion had moved from disdain to affection, but watching them in slow motion I felt deep admiration for them. Little brown jobs indeed: they are magnificent – a prince among birds.

CHAPTER TEN

A Recipe for Scrambled Eggs

WHEN I WAS ABOUT TEN, my parents decided to foster my growing interest in animals by giving me a book with a title something like *Amazing Facts from Nature*. I repaid their kindness by tormenting them with interminable questions from it. What is the oldest living thing on earth? Where is the deepest spot in the ocean? How many hens' eggs would it take to fill an ostrich egg? Only this last has ever proved useful.

Armed with this half-remembered bit of useless information, I went into the shop and bought ninety eggs. It looked great on the expense claim when I got home, especially since the next entry read 'Three ostrich eggs'. These had been tastefully painted up with the words 'Souvenir of

Kenya'. The shopping trip was completed with 'One bottle of washing-up liquid' and 'One small funnel'.

In the middle of most action-films the hero assembles an odd assortment of household goods which he then uses to make a bomb or some complicated timing device. As I unpacked and set to work on my shopping, I felt like a comic version of that hero. First I scrubbed off the 'Souvenir of Kenya'. Then with an electric drill, I enlarged the holes that had been used to blow the eggs.

The recipe then read as follows:

Whisk together two and a half dozen eggs.

Empty the bottle of washing-up liquid, and wash out the bottle.

Pour the whisked eggs through the funnel into the washing-up bottle.

Squirt the egg mixture into the cleaned ostrich egg.

When full, seal up the holes at the ends of the ostrich egg with Araldite.

Repeat for the remaining eggs, and serve.

'Serving' involved rather more than the recipe implies because this feast was not intended for any run-of-the-mill diners. The gourmets I was hoping to tempt were Egyptian vultures, and the best place to find and film them is the Nairobi National Park. Getting there was easier than it sounds, because I had made all my preparations in Nairobi, and the park is only an hour's drive from the city.

Egyptian vultures aren't simply big scavenging birds that happen to live in Egypt, they are a separate species, indeed the smallest of the vultures. They have dirty white plumage and are bald along the whole of their neck right up to the top of their head. On the ground all vultures are scruffy, dirty and clumsy, and Egyptian vultures are no exception. They are ungainly and look thoroughly disreputable, but when they take to the air they are transformed into true beauties with huge wings and their supreme ability to soar on the gentlest of air currents. Unfortunately, I was wanting to film them on the ground, so I would have to make the best I could of scruffy, dishevelled earthbound vultures.

Being the smallest of the various species of vulture, Egyptians fare rather badly at a kill, because they are chased and bullied by all the others. Perhaps this is why they have evolved a trick that no other bird can manage. They can eat ostrich eggs. Other vultures and most other animals have no success with these giant eggs: next to nothing else can crack them open. They are so strong that a full-grown man can stand on an ostrich egg without breaking it – another amazing fact that I learned from my childhood book.

An Egyptian vulture uses a remarkable technique to break ostrich eggs. When it sees one, the vulture picks up a stone, walks over to the egg, and drops the stone. Occasionally the stone hits and cracks the egg, giving the vulture a fine feast. Egyptian vultures have evolved this complicated bit of behaviour so they do it instinctively: it's not a trick that individuals have to learn. This strange behaviour evolved because ostriches also behave rather oddly: they tend to leave their eggs lying around abandoned and unprotected. Most animals are very careful to look after their offspring, but ostriches have adopted what seems like a cavalier attitude to their eggs and it follows directly from their unusual breeding behaviour.

Ostriches may seem natural comics, but during the breeding season, males fight for territory, and these battles may last for an hour or more. A territory holder proclaims ownership of his kingdom by strutting around and waving his wings up and down. On the occasions when he really wants to emphasise the fact that he's boss, he sits down, fluffs out his feathers and starts flagging his head violently from side to side. This head-waving gets more and more energetic, and, to underline his territorial claim, the male's neck blushes bright red making a livid contrast with his black and white plumage. With each swipe of his head, he also releases a deep breathy grunt till the whole spectacle rises to a paroxysm of righteous ownership that other ostriches have to take seriously. To my eyes the entire performance only makes an ostrich look more comical than he did before, but he doesn't do it for my benefit.

If the full performance of the territory-owner's display fails to repel an invader, owner and challenger set off on a long distance high-speed chase across the grassland. With their high stepping gait they move up through the ranks of comics to rival John Cleese and his Ministry of Silly Walks. I did see one chase end in actual fighting, but usually one animal or the other gives up exhausted. Occasionally, the two running males stray outside the resident's territory, at which point he turns tail and heads home. It's dramatic, as well as entertaining stuff, and I had great fun filming it.

Trying to follow racing ostriches and film them as they ran, we clocked over 80 kph, so they really cover the ground. For Kilonzo, my driver, this was quite the best part of the job, and when we spotted a racing pair, there was no holding him. He would set off across the grassland with a whoop, and that was the sign for me to hang on for dear life. Perfectly flat areas became rutted as we raced towards them. Hitting an invisible game track produced enough of a jolt to boost me to lift-off velocity, and when a wheel found an elephant's footprint I was shaken till I felt like a rat in a terrier's jaws. After the first of these death defying chases I took to strapping myself in and I learned to brace myself with elbows and knees, but the little four-wheel drive bucked and tossed so violently that I still spent most of the chase somewhere between the seat and the roof. Next I tried hooking one foot under my seat, and bracing the other against the dashboard, but I merely looked like a contorted octopus. Whatever I did I shook like a cartoon character for the duration of the chase. Trying to film through the window at the same time was laughable.

After a few bruising attempts to get the shot, my lacerated scalp told me that the greatest danger came from head-butting the roof. The solution came in the shape of a great stack of foam held to the top of my head with sticky tape leaving me looking like some post-modern socialite en route to Ascot. To begin with, my headwear worked as a padded crash helmet, but with time it grew till in its final incarnation, the multicoloured foam was stacked up to about twenty-five centimetres. That way it filled the entire gap between my head and the car roof, so I was firmly wedged into my seat. It helped and eventually we got the shot, but I doubt my head-dress will ever really catch on as a fashion item.

A male ostrich's territorial display is part of his breeding effort, but even when he has established his territory he still has to court his potential mates, and ostrich courtship is as unusual as their fighting. For a start it's the male who makes a nest. He does little more than make a scrape in the sandy soil, but it's enough. Once he's made his nest, a territorial male attracts females to it with more fluffing up of his feathers and head-waving.

Females behave in one of two ways. Some females wander from one territory to another, to be courted by the resident male of each territory they come into. These itinerant females mate with a succession of males, and lay their eggs in several nests. Other females are faithful to a single male, only mate with him, and, at least for that season, they lay all their eggs in his nest. The result is that there may be dozens of eggs laid by several different females in one nest.

The male and the resident females then incubate, but there are often far more eggs in the nest than a bird can cover, so only some of them are kept at the right temperature. The resident females lay their eggs later than their wandering sisters, and they lay in the centre of the clutch, so it is the fickle females whose eggs tend to get left out in the cold. These eggs are pushed away from the nest and they make a huge food resource for the few animals that can use it. Cue Egyptian vultures.

It seemed a long shot, but I was trying to film Egyptian vultures picking up stones and dropping them on ostrich eggs. As if this behaviour wasn't improbable enough, I had one small additional problem. The producer had got me out to Kenya to film a number of things, and the Egyptian vultures were not the top priority for me on that trip. The timing was a compromise, and the vulture sequence had not been the one to determine the dates. In other words, I was in Kenya at totally the wrong time of year for that sequence. Ostrich courtship, egg-laying and hatching had all happened months earlier, which is why I had had to recreate ostrich eggs from souvenirs. But I consoled myself with the fact that at least there wasn't a glut of eggs at the time, and any vulture I managed to find wouldn't be suffering from a surfeit of ostrich eggs. Whether they would even think about dropping stones on them was an open question, but there was only one way to find out.

Once in the park, the first relevant thing Kilonzo and I spotted was a troupe of baboons. They looked like good candidates for the role of 'Animals that are unable to get into ostrich eggs', so I carefully placed the eggs in their path, and retreated to the car to film them. Amazingly they obliged and failed to get into my ostrich eggs. They rolled them about, picked them up and tried to stretch their considerable jaws round them, but to no effect. It all looked great through the lens, so a happy cameraman collected his undamaged eggs when the baboons had passed.

To my amazement we soon spotted an Egyptian vulture quite close to the track. This seemed like ridiculously good luck, but sometimes things just do go right. From the car, I worked out where to put the eggs so that I could have a clear view of them and have some bushes in the background. If I was going to manipulate my vulture, I might as well make it look as good as possible.

The park guards are extremely vigilant at keeping visitors inside their cars, so I scanned the horizon before quietly climbing out of the car. First I collected some stones from the track: I wanted to make things as easy as possible for the bird. Give it to him on a plate, I thought. The vulture just watched as I slowly carried the eggs plus the stones to the selected spot. I carefully put down the eggs, and started scattering the stones.

I stood up, almost ready to go back to the car, and had two revelations in quick succession. The first explained why the vulture was there, and this was the easy one. I spotted the carcass of a wildebeest lying near the bushes about five metres from me. My second revelation explained why the carcass of a wildebeest happened to be there, and this was slightly more interesting. One member of the pride of lions that had killed the wildebeest came out of the bushes to watch me.

I have never had great ambitions as an Olympic athlete, but I changed my mind the moment I saw that lion. My training started there and then. I dropped the rest of my stones and ran as I had never run before.

From the safety of the passenger seat, and with the door slammed shut I could look at my lion appreciatively. He was big, and I was very glad that I was watching him from inside the car. Slowly I realised that there was a roaring noise and it wasn't coming from the lion. Nor was it the blood rushing through my ears: it was Kilonzo howling with laughter. I joined him, and the lion watched us disdainfully, as only lions can.

Then it was waiting time, but now the lions were on my side. They pulled the carcass under the bushes, which left my poor little vulture without his meal. And bless him, he did his little trick. He picked up one of my hastily scattered stones, and dropped it on one of the eggs. Suddenly his scruffiness left him. He repeated his performance and I was filming away with great glee. He had become a noble beast, with his fine creamy plumes waving gently in the sun. And what an imperious head he had. Intelligently and deftly he picked up more stones to drop on my eggs. I loved him.

Unfortunately he never managed to crack an egg and gain his just reward, so at about midday he flew off. That was when optimism and ambition got the better of me. I decided to hang on in the hope that one of the lions would oblige and complete the story beyond my wildest dreams. Lions are just about the only animal other than an Egyptian vulture that can crack ostrich eggs. Their gape is so huge that they can get an egg into their jaws and just crush it. If one of them would saunter over and crack an ostrich egg it would make a perfect end to a memorable day.

So we sat in the car, and the lions sat under their bush about thirty metres away. For that entire afternoon they showed no sign of activity. Kilonzo and I ate our lunch but the lions just lay there. Only lions and large reptiles can manage total inactivity for a long period of time, and these lions did just that. They showed absolutely no interest in the dead wildebeest or the eggs till, as the sun was sinking and starting to lose its strength, one of them stood up, stretched and sauntered over towards the eggs.

I still think I was cruelly unlucky. If only that dopey old lion had made it over to the eggs five minutes earlier, I would have got a totally memorable, world-class shot. As it was, just after the lion stood up and just before he reached the eggs, I realised where I had gone wrong in preparing the eggs. I had taken great care to stop any of the whisked egg seeping out of the holes in the shell: even a dribble of egg might have given the baboons both motive and opportunity to keep working on an egg and eventually crack it open. No that would never do; so I had sealed them hermetically with the Araldite.

By five o'clock my ostrich eggs had been sitting out in the tropical sun for the better part of a day, and the scrambled egg inside had started to ferment. The pressure in that egg must have been rising for some time, but because I had done such a good job of sealing the holes I am proud to say that neither gas nor fermenting scrambled egg escaped.

When eventually the inevitable happened it was hard to tell who was the most surprised, Kilonzo, myself or the lion. The first egg went off like a grenade, and we all jumped. Fragments of splintered shell clattered down like shrapnel all around us but for a while I had no idea what had happened. When the second egg detonated a few minutes later all became clear.

At the first blast, our valiant lion turned tail and scuttled back to the bushes about as fast as I had scuttled back to the car earlier. Kilonzo and I were both speechless with laughter, but I still have fantasies about the shot that nearly was.

In my imagination, a brave noble lion approaches an innocent looking egg, gently picks it up and starts to close its mighty jaws in anticipation of a tasty snack. Suddenly the egg explodes blowing shell out of the lion's mouth and the king of the jungle retreats retching and vomiting with egg all over his face. Oh so near.

CHAPTER ELEVEN

Gorilla Tactics

WHEN IT COMES TO MANIPULATING wild animals, we filmmakers are mere beginners. To play sophisticated tricks on a wild animal takes a very thorough understanding of the species plus a great deal of time, and we are rarely in a position to do that much spadework. So we often try to find a friendly person who has been working with the animals for a long time, and that usually means an academic.

Among academics there is one group that stands head and shoulders above all others in this respect: the people I am thinking of are primatologists. So for instance, it was well over a year before Dianne Fossey could get near enough to her gorillas to record what they were doing, and it took Jane Goodall about the same amount of time before she could really start work on her chimpanzees. Habituating wild primates just does take that long, and although the process is described as 'habituation', I would argue that it consists of manipulating the animals into accepting humans as safe visitors.

Thanks to the help of academics, several films have been made about wild primates, and my own film about gibbons is a good example of this since it would have been impossible to make it without the help of Warren Brockleman and his habituated group. This sounds as though filmmakers are parasites riding on the backs of academics, and we certainly rely on them in many ways, but it's not totally one-sided. Having their research filmed for television is a great way for academics to reach a wider audience than their usual journals, and publicity helps them in their endless quest for funding.

Today there are numerous habituated primates groups being studied, and there are one or two species that have passed beyond being the exclusive preserve of researchers and filmmakers, to become tourist attractions. In these species, one or two groups have been so well habituated that they can be visited regularly, and the fees that tourists pay contribute to the protection of the animals. Recently I filmed one of these primate groups, and it marked a high point in my life with animals.

We joined the tourist party, and since there were four of us, two researchers named Ian Redmon and Liz Williamson, Robin the producer, and myself, we took up most of the six places permitted for that day's visit. The reserve manager gave us a brief pep talk and asked each one of us if we were suffering from any illness such as a cold that we could pass on to the animals because if so we should not go. He also told us that if at any time we felt threatened, the thing to do was to look away from the animal and lie down.

With these words fresh in our minds, we set off just after dawn from the main gate of the reserve with a tracker and two guides carrying ancient AK47s. If these were intended to reassure us they failed – in my case they had the opposite effect since guns always make me nervous.

For two hours we tramped through dripping forest up the side of the beautiful volcanoes that mark the boundary between Uganda and the Congo. We went up and down. Up was where we were trying to go: down is where we kept sliding. Eventually our tracker stopped to examine a clearing in the trees.

'They were here last night,' he said. 'They are near.'

He soon found the direction the group had taken, and, to be honest, their path was so clear that even I could spot the trail of trampled vegetation and broken twigs. Another ten minutes and our tracker signalled for us to stay where we were and keep quiet while he went forward to see if he could spot anything. He soon reappeared through the wall of vegetation and announced that our journey was over.

'They are behind these trees.' He was whispering this time. 'Come slowly. Sit down when you see them.'

One by one we pushed our way through a final curtain of trees and scanned the little clearing. Suddenly I spotted a movement and at that instant I found myself face to face with one of my ancestors. It was like looking into a distorting mirror because in the middle of the clearing, looking straight back at me was a mountain gorilla.

I never set much store by first impressions, but on this occasion, I think I got it about right. Quite simply I found myself looking at the most fascinating animal I had ever seen. It was love at first sight. Every limb, every movement, every gesture intrigued me. This animal was so familiar, and yet so different that I just had to keep watching.

By contrast, the gorilla seemed to find me profoundly boring. Every day, at about this time, a troupe of humans clattered and crashed their way through the forest and then just sat and looked. So, once she had worked out the composition of today's troupe of camera toting humans, she largely ignored us and quietly got on with the day's chores.

'We have one hour from now,' said the guard who was sitting behind me with his Kalashnikov across his knees.

I knew immediately that it wasn't going to be enough time, so I went back to watching my cousin. The gorilla I had spotted first was a smallish female, but this only became apparent when the dominant male of the group, the silverback, sauntered into view the other side of the clearing. He was about fifteen metres away, but he was so imposing that every eye, human and gorilla, followed him. He had shoulders on him that wouldn't have been out of place in an American Football team, except that he didn't need the padding, and unlike those over-sized and professionally violent humans, these lovely pacific creatures gave no hint of aggression. They were mild and gentle, and I doubt that any of their human visitors felt intimidated at all. I really couldn't tear my eyes away from them. I was surely looking at the finest animal I had ever seen, and the ultimate habituated animal.

Beside me I noticed that Ian was making odd grunting noises and looking down at a handful of leaves he was screwing up and tearing. The gorillas glanced at us occasionally, but spent most of their time ignoring us. I guessed that Ian had to be copying polite gorilla behaviour and trying to make himself and indeed all of us welcome by displaying his perfect manners. Then I noticed that Liz and our tracker were also playing with some leaves, so I joined in as well.

'That's right,' whispered Liz, 'make little grunts and look at the ground. That's what they do when they're happy. They'll relax quicker if they think we're calm.'

'Much more relaxed and they'll fall asleep,' I whispered back to her, but I was wrong because slowly their behaviour did change and they started wandering about a bit more, eating and grooming each other. Soon they too were making the little grunting noises, and I felt we had persuaded them that we were well brought up and knew how to behave properly.

'I think we ought to do a bit of filming soon,' said Robin beside me. Producers are like that – no soul. To be fair, he had spent thousands of pounds getting us here, and I had already spent fully ten of our permitted sixty minutes just gazing.

'James, can you sort out a good spot to put Ian and Liz so that you can get a shot of them with the gorillas in the background?'

He was right, this was the shot to start on, so reluctantly I tore my eyes away from those wonderful animals and set to work. Filming the two researchers with the gorillas was the central shot we had come here to get because Liz and Ian had some important things to say about the animals we were watching. Above all, they needed to say that the animals we were looking at made up the one and only troupe of wild mountain gorillas that anybody could visit anywhere in the world with reasonable safety.

This point was key to the programme we were making. It wasn't so much about the lives of mountain gorillas: it was more concerned with their plight during the terrible events that had recently rocked this part of Africa. We were actually in Uganda, but Uganda, Congo and Rwanda all meet somewhere near where we were, and alas, mountain gorillas only live in these mountains. We were there a year or so after the worst of the atrocities, but although the fighting between Hutu and Tutsi had left the front pages of the world's press, there were still tens of thousands of armed men roaming the mountains and thousands of scores to be settled. Millions had been massacred in this area during the years before our visit, and the hatred had not died with the departure of the journalists. As if to confirm this, we heard several bursts of distant gunfire while we were in the forest though fortunately it remained distant.

Gorilla Tactics

This awful background gave an added dimension to our time with the gorillas, but I must confess that I found it all too easy to ignore the horrors of the political situation: the animals were so wonderful. What made it even more amazing was the fact that nobody had been able to sit and watch gorillas like this till Dianne Fossey habituated a group of them during the late sixties. So, it has only been for about forty years that humans and gorillas had been able to meet peaceably as we were doing. For a brief time during the nineties there had been three or four habituated groups that tourists could pay to go and watch, and visitors had queued up to see them. However, following the fighting and the atrocities, those other gorilla groups were all in hideously unsafe areas, so visits to them had been stopped.

We managed to get a whole series of shots of Liz and Ian with the gorillas, so Robin was happy. The close-up shots of the two researchers talking we could do later somewhere else in the forest because we didn't need the gorillas in the background for that. At last I could turn my attention back to the animals themselves. But no sooner had I spotted a nice close-up of the silver-back than Kalashnikov announced that we had five minutes left.

We left the troupe in near silence, but as soon as we were a little way from them, an outburst of excited chatter broke from all of us. Did you see this? Did you notice that? Did you see the baby using its mother as a trampoline? We all behaved like six-year-olds at a birthday party and it seemed totally appropriate.

Ian and Liz were particularly curious to see how Robin

and I would react to the encounter. They had both dedicated years of their lives to gorillas, and they both thought of gorillas as friends. However, they seemed to expect us to be on a totally different wavelength from them, and be rather blasé about meeting just another species of animal. I could honestly tell them that I had been blown away by the experience, and couldn't wait to go back the next day.

Liz was also excited as we left the gorillas, but she was agitated and almost in tears, which surprised me. I knew that she had spent the last four years in Rwanda working on the group of animals originally habituated by Dianne Fossey, and I suppose I expected her to be sufficiently familiar with gorillas for the full impact of meeting them to have worn off.

Later that day, we filmed Liz and Ian talking about the gorillas' plight, and slowly it became clear why she was so moved at seeing these gorillas here in Uganda. Liz had been confined to her camp in Rwanda for a year and a half because it was too dangerous for her to go into the forest, so these were the first gorillas she had seen in all that time. She had no idea what had happened to her own gorilla friends, and seeing these ones brought it all back to her.

That evening I learned more about our situation, and the added news did nothing to make it any more comfortable. Apparently, about six weeks before our visit, a party of tourists visiting another troupe of habituated gorillas in the Congo had been kidnapped, and several of them were subsequently murdered. Nobody had been allowed to visit that group since the kidnapping, but somehow I failed to spot the story in the newspapers before we came.

I wasn't particularly concerned, but Robin still wanted to reassure me, or maybe he wanted to encourage himself. 'That was in the Congo, and things there are much worse than here. We're not going near the Congo. In fact the special insurance we took out lays down that we are not to go within three kilometres of the Congo border. And we'll stick to that. OK?'

That was fine by me. My only worry was that this was the first I'd heard about special insurance, and it set me thinking. Did it cover flying in the SAS to free us? Was it to cover ransoms? Or was it just death benefit?

The next day we set off to visit the gorillas again, and repeated much the same slipping slithering climb as the day before. Eventually we found them, and this time I was able to concentrate on filming the animals rather than Ian and Liz. They came even closer to us than they had on the first day, and my love for them was well and truly sealed. Unfortunately, one of the things that Robin wanted was film showing the injuries that two or three of them had suffered. One mother was particularly poignant because she was valiantly looking after a young baby despite having lost a hand. She had nothing but a stump on the one arm, but was very adept at holding her squirming offspring none the less.

'What happened to her?' I asked Ian.

'Land mine. Trap. Could be either. It's hard to tell whether her injury's from the war or the poachers.'

'Is poaching a big problem?' I asked.

'Terrible. Bush meat is what people call it, and a gorilla yields a lot of bush meat. It's worth a lot of money.'

'They kill gorillas for the meat?' I asked appalled.

'Oh yes.'

Now that I had met the gorillas, and fallen in love with them, this sounded almost like cannibalism, so I had to probe and find out more about it. 'Which is the bigger problem for the gorillas, soldiers or poachers?' I asked.

'Soldiers, poachers, they're all one,' replied Ian. 'Hungry soldiers will happily eat gorilla if they can find one to shoot. And there are thousands of armed men in these hills. If they see movement they shoot. Habituated animals are particularly at risk because they're less likely to run away from approaching guerrillas.' It was a chilling pun that I had been very keen to avoid.

Ian's comment highlighted a danger inherent in habituating animals that had never really occurred to me. If these were the ultimate habituated animals, their plight cast a huge shadow over the whole idea of habituating wild animals. It is quite possible that habituating these gorillas increased their risk of being shot by armed militia, and that is a heavy responsibility that could outweigh the benefits of people being able to know more about them.

As we left the gorillas that day I happened to ask one of the guides a naïve question. 'How far is it to the frontier do you think?'

'It is that ridge. Just there.' He pointed to a rocky outcrop about fifty metres away.

'So that's the Congo?'

'Oh yes.'

'Let's get out of here,' said Robin.

CHAPTER TWELVE

Weasel Words

IMAGINE YOU ARE TRYING TO film a beetle. It's an average size beetle, an ordinary beetle-shaped beetle and a reasonably common species at that. So it's nothing very special, and you're fairly confident about filming it because you have often seen the beetle you are after in a patch of woodland you know well. So you take your camera and go to your patch of woodland where you find your beetle reasonably quickly, but it scurries away the moment you see it. You manage to find it again, but you lose it again. You find it again, lose it again, find it again and so on. You probably go round that loop for quite a while.

When eventually you manage to corner your beetle, the fun can really start. There he is, you can see him quite easily; he's down on the ground and you're standing right next to him. But if you're going to get a decent shot of him, it's no good having the camera up where you are and looking down. You need to be with him at ground level where you can look at him head on and show your viewer what the world looks like from a beetle's point of view. So very slowly you lower your camera down on the ground, trying desperately not to scare your beetle. You need the camera on a roughly horizontal bit of ground and it's best to avoid putting it in a puddle because a wet camera costs over a thousand pounds to repair.

It must be your lucky day because you manage to position the camera safely, and your beetle is still in sight. That's good, but it's a bit early to start celebrating: you still haven't tried looking through the viewfinder. When you do, you discover that you have put the camera right by a patch of nettles that gently caress your cheek, and the dead log you hoped would form an attractive background is actually all you can see.

Within minutes, you are scuttling about on hands and knees like a demented crab, and the whole scene degenerates into slapstick. You kneel on a thorn. You flinch and hit your head on an overhanging branch, which makes the beetle take fright and scuttle off. As you crawl after him your hands get filthy, and you smear mud on your precious camera. You find yourself lying in something rank and slimy, which is probably what the beetle was eating before you disturbed him.

Every time your beetle moves, you have to move yourself plus your camera, and the upheaval is quite enough to frighten a torpid snail, let alone a beetle. The more you chase him, the more you scare the poor creature, so he runs faster, he runs farther and he buries himself deeper. If you do ever manage to get everything right and you're ready to take a shot, you run up against an immutable law of nature. The sun is obliged to choose that precise moment to go behind a cloud.

In the studio I have muted classical music playing: I find Bach best for filming beetles. I can take my time and carefully make myself a miniature set, rather like a stage or film set, but in this case designed to look like the inside of a pile of leaves rather than the banqueting hall of a palace. I then use a trick that feature-film directors might consider when working with particularly temperamental Hollywood actors. I enclose my set with high clear plastic walls, to stop my star escaping, and incidentally, 'star' is the right word because a beetle can be as temperamental as any diva. Finally, I put my whole construction, beetle, set and enclosure, on a table. Now, instead of scrabbling through the undergrowth, the camera and I are both at a reasonable working height, and it is relatively easy to get the camera pointing at the beetle. I replace the sun with a selection of lights to create the moody lighting that I imagine you find inside a pile of leaves, and clouds become a horrid memory.

You might think that I am trying to design a world for my comfort: a world in which I can put my backside on a chair rather than stick it up in the air. Or perhaps I come across as a control freak who enjoys playing God. I think both interpretations miss the point. With almost everything under control, I no longer have to pursue my beetle. I can put him into the set where he can settle down and become familiar with his new space. I can adjust his new environment to suit him: the right temperature, his favourite food (although that can involve more than you bargained for), the Brandenberg Concertos. You can get everything just right for you and the beetle, and then he might – he just might – given time – start to behave naturally, which will mean that I have a chance of filming him properly. So you are confronted with a wonderful paradox. By cheating outrageously and putting your animal into a totally unnatural set, you are more likely to film natural behaviour than by trying to film him in his natural surroundings.

Only when you add animals to your carefully constructed set do you discover its limitations. Animals that have been gently wandering about suddenly grow springs in their legs and leap over towering sheets of plastic. Reasonable size animals shrink and vanish into cracks that expand to accommodate them. Animals that specialise in camouflage disappear entirely. Normally docile, sedentary animals become gravity-defying rock-climbers that scale vertical walls. As a result, I've chased frogs across the floors of numerous studios. I've lost mice in many more and I've spent ages trying to rescue insects that have flown off in an attempt to commit ritual suicide on the lights.

The very worst animal for testing a set made its presence known to me as I walked towards my line of live mouse-traps. One of the traps jumped in the air, did a somersault, landed, flipped over and rolled down the bank. I grabbed the trap, loosened the catch on it, and dropped the whole thing into the sack I had with me. I immediately tied the sack as tightly as I could. I was pretty quick, but it was a close-run thing because before I had the string tied, the creature had escaped from the trap and was swirling around wildly. I refer to it as a creature in the singular, but to judge by the way the sack was flapping about, it could well have held half a dozen miniature monkeys that had decided to practise tag wrestling.

I went straight home and emptied the contents of my sack into a set I had prepared several weeks earlier. It was the most secure set I had ever made with high, inward sloping clear plastic walls. On top of the walls I had a lid and on top of the lid I had put a heavy weight. It was my miniature Alcatraz, and I told myself that even a poltergeist couldn't get out of it.

And what was all the fuss about? How would I explain my jumping trap and writhing sack without invoking magic? The answer was a weasel. I had had dealings with weasels before, so I knew what a jumping trap implied. I also knew that you can't be too careful when dealing with a weasel. When I caught my first one, I put on some heavy leather gloves, and tried to extract the animal from the trap. Holding a well-greased eel would have been easier. Within seconds I had lost the weasel and quite a lot of blood. A weasel's teeth have no respect for heavy leather gloves.

A weasel is about twenty centimetres long, which means that one could easily sit in the palm of a hand (I'm still looking for a volunteer to demonstrate this). At that size it is one of the smallest members of the family that includes animals like mink, ferrets and mongooses. They are all fiercely carnivorous and move with the dynamic grace that ballerinas aspire to. I have never seen a weasel walk. They streak about with a dizzying turn of speed, and total unpredictability. They are not big animals, but they are pure energy.

A weasel's idea of heaven must be a dry-stone wall, because it can insinuate itself between the stones and pop up unexpectedly to catch spiders, beetles or baby mice. This was handy because it was exactly what I wanted to film. I was making a programme about a dry-stone wall for the BBC, and I thought that including a weasel would liven up the story a bit.

My weasel set was quite a simple one consisting of nothing more than a stone wall with some grass in front of it. As soon as I had put my sack into the set and had the lid on firmly, I sat down and waited patiently for my Houdini to get out of the sack. I must have waited for about three milliseconds. I imagine that firing a bullet in a steel lined room would produce an effect rather like releasing that weasel. He just streaked about, ricocheting off everything so fast that within two minutes he had explored the whole area. He was up and down, left, right, in, out – everywhere. How was I going to film this thing? There had to be some way to slow him down. So I turned down the lights and crept out of the room.

About half an hour later, I tiptoed back and had a peep through the viewfinder. I was desperately keen to keep quiet for fear of alarming my weasel, but my plan went the way of most good resolutions when I started to splutter with suppressed giggles. Having exhausted the set, my little weasel had decided that the only thing that held any interest was the camera lens: boredom is a real problem for such an intelligent animal. He must have done a pole vault to reach my lens, but when I looked through the viewfinder, there he was, looking straight back at me. He was hanging onto the bottom edge of the lens-hood and looked just like a cartoon character peering over a wall. He was probably trying to check that I had the exposure right.

He calmed down after a few days, and I managed to get some shots of him weaving his way between the stones. It was very attractive, but it wasn't enough. I wanted him to inject excitement into the programme, and he wasn't really doing that. I wanted drama and that usually means hunting, but the very idea of trying to film this bit of animated lightning while it went hunting was enough to give me nightmares.

I wanted the drama without headache, so I needed to take full advantage of the fact that I was working with an animal in a set. In other words, I was going to have to fake the hunt. First I tried making a dummy mouse, a precursor of the one we used with the cat in Australia. The weasel looked interested for a split second, and then just ignored my creation. I tried putting some bedding from a mouse nest into the set, and he sniffed around it briefly before dashing off to investigate something else. He was much too smart to be fooled by anything like that. I obviously needed the real thing, but that was easier said than done.

After several days of trying different tricks, I found myself walking away from the studio when I spotted our cat, Charlie, hunting in the garden, and an evil little thought came to me. He was watching a mouse hole. For a while, only the tip of his tail moved. Then there was the telltale wiggle of his bottom, a slight tensing of his shoulders and he pounced. A tragic little squeal greeted his efforts, and he looked around him.

Now it was my turn to stalk the cat. Looking at a point several metres to his left, I sidled up towards him. I pounced but needless to say, Charlie was long-gone by the time I reached the grass, but my fingers closed on the tiny corpse of the mouse. A livid cat watched me from a few metres away, but I didn't care.

I went back to the studio, put the little corpse behind a clump of grass in the weasel's set and got ready to film him. Cautiously he peeped out from his lair in among the rocks and for a third time a predator pounced on the mouse. The difference was that the weasel really proved his mettle. Blood flew everywhere as he tore the mouse to bits and bolted the whole lot down in seconds flat. I filmed the entire performance, and it made an excellent little sequence although the editor did cut out some of the more gory moments for fear of disturbing the audience.

A few years later, a producer asked me to film a weasel again. Being slightly older and wiser, I mentioned that there might be a small problem.

'No problem,' came the reply. 'I've managed to track down an academic who's doing research on weasels, and he's got a pet one. We can borrow it for a few days.' Great. That could bring the job a little closer to sanity.

'What do you want me to film it doing?'

'I need a chase sequence. You know, a weasel chasing a mouse. I'm not after the kill, just the hunting sequence.'

'Oh come off it,' was the closest I could get to a polite answer: I knew a bit about hunting sequences with weasels. 'I can do you a weasel feeding, but a weasel hunting is a nightmare. For one thing the action is going to happen in milliseconds. It's also bound to happen in a corner of the set where I can't film it. And thirdly, it's illegal to put a weasel and a mouse into a set together. So no.'

'No, no, no. All I want is some shots of the mouse in the set, you know the sort of stuff, just scuttling about and being mousy. Then you take the mouse out and put the weasel in. Get a few shots of him in the same spots. We can cut them together in the edit and it'll be a classic chase sequence.'

That was making a bit of sense, so I agreed to give it a go.

'Oh by the way,' he added, 'I've also managed to find a guy who is researching field mice, and he's got a tame one. All these academics seem to need to keep their study animals as pets. Perhaps they just don't see enough of them in the wild. Anyway it should be easy.' Famous last words.

Both the weasel and the field mouse arrived, and I made a handsome set for them. First I put the mouse in and that was rather a shock. Field mice are not like their domestic cousins. They are much more timorous, neurotic and just plain skittish, so I was amazed to see this mouse stroll around the set. He wandered about as if he owned it. He was one very cool mouse.

The weasel was also placid by weasel standards, but that said, he was much more of a handful to film than the mouse. Even after I had given him a few days to calm down, he was still leaving scorch marks as he raced around the set. But eventually I managed to get some film of both of them, and sent it all off to the lab.

A couple of weeks later I visited the editing room to see how they were getting on.

'Look at this,' said the editor. He sat the producer and me down in front of one of the viewing machines and put the film on.

What we watched had us both in stitches. There was the weasel dashing around like a bundle of nerves. Enter the mouse, casual, stylish and well in control. Another quick flash of the weasel followed by the languid mouse. Once again we saw a wired weasel and a mellow mouse. The sequence lasted about a minute, and it was fine, except for one thing. The mouse was chasing the weasel.

'It only works that way round,' said the editor, and he was right. Think of any feature film chase sequence: the pursued is the one that has to look terrified while the pursuer is meant to look as though he is coolly in control of the situation, and my weasel and my mouse had switched roles.

'See if you can get me something so that I can have the weasel chasing the mouse. Please.'

That took a bit of doing, but eventually I discovered that when he was really well fed, the weasel slowed down a bit. He didn't slow down much, and he was only mellow for a matter of moments before he took himself off to have a sleep. But for those few minutes my weasel behaved a bit more like a normal animal and I managed to get enough film to make the editor reasonably happy. At the time I felt I had scored a victory, but in hindsight I'm not so sure. I dearly love weasels, but I don't honestly think I ever managed better than a draw with one.

CHAPTER THIRTEEN

Bamboo and Beer

'CAN YOU JUST GET HER to come down that slope, behind the big tree and along the track to my right,' I asked. I was having a great time. I was being a film director, and the very idea of being able to direct an animal was heaven. Arranging for it to go where I wanted was giving me a serious power complex, and I was revelling in it.

There was a shouted translation into Mandarin from Ken my interpreter. Explanations followed, with a series of people saying, 'Ready?', 'OK', and then, 'Action'. No matter where you go, everybody knows that filming involves people shouting 'Action.'

I set the camera going, and one of the keepers, Mr. Chan, walked along the route I had identified, carrying a stick of sugar cane. I let him go out of frame and followed instead the animal that was pursuing him. It was a giant panda. She came trundling down the slope, behind the tree and along the track where she went nicely out of frame just as I wanted.

I turned the camera off and smiled smugly. I was very aware that if I had been trying to film wild animals, I would have had to wait for months to get even that simple shot of a panda walking through the forest, so I felt very comfortable about what I was doing. Despite the obvious advantages of using captives, I normally prefer to film wild animals, and have stringent criteria for when it is right to resort to captive ones. But if anything meets those criteria it has to be pandas. There are so few of them left that they have become synonymous with rarity among animals, they live in extremely inaccessible places and they are so shy that even glimpsing one in the wild makes a red letter day. No, captive pandas were the only answer. Once the beginning of my shot was edited away, Mr. Chan and his sugar cane would disappear, and the viewer would just see a panda moving through her natural habitat, with the mountains behind her.

Those mountains of Szechwan form the northern flank of the Himalayas and it was the first time I had been in that part of the world. The hills are thickly forested and incised by deep rocky rivers that hurl themselves down from the higher mountains. Behind every ridge there is a higher one, and we could see this endless march rise to the snow covered peaks of the Himalayas proper. And this is the only place where pandas survive in the wild: they could hardly have chosen anywhere more beautiful.

The panda is, of course, the world-wide symbol for conservation, which means that there is a great deal written on them and their plight, so it was quite easy to read up about them before I left home. I learned for instance that despite enormous effort, there are only a few hundred of them left in the mountains. At one time poaching was a problem, but this has been considerably reduced, perhaps because the penalty for killing a panda in China may be death. Most wild pandas now live in the reserves that have been established for their benefit, and they seem to be just about hanging on.

Wo Long, one of the biggest reserves, includes the panda-breeding centre, where I was based. About a dozen pandas are kept there, and as the name implies, the justification for keeping them in captivity is that the staff are trying to get them to breed. Pandas are famously bad at breeding, or, to put it another way, nobody has yet worked out the conditions they need for breeding. As a species they seem to have taken a group decision to become extinct. The people at the breeding centre do everything they can think of to frustrate this collective death wish, but it's uphill work. While I was there I watched and filmed some of their work, including one day when the vets extracted semen from an anaesthetised male, and then tried to inseminate a female artificially. It looked painful and unpleasant, and although they have had some success, their programme has produced very few baby pandas.

The animal I was filming was Qian-Qian, and she was one of the females involved in the breeding programme.

Most of the animals there had repeated double-barrelled names like hers because such names are a sign of deep respect in Chinese, and pandas are seen as very important animals. Qian-Qian was the regular film star among the captive animals, because she could be relied on to perform properly. That was what I was told anyway. She knew the ropes, I was told, and I believed them as she obligingly followed Mr. Chan and his sticks of sugar cane. He gave her occasional bits of it to keep her interested, and everything was going rather well.

A panda eating sugar cane was a concept I could handle, after all, it's pretty much like bamboo, only sweeter, but a panda eating meat? That really came as a surprise. While I was in Wo Long I learned that in the wild they regularly eat things like nesting birds, and even carrion, though nothing in the literature had warned me about that. A still bigger shock was the realisation that pandas are not quite the sweet cuddly animals they appear to be. Only a week before I filmed Qian-Qian, there had been a photo opportunity for some celebrity or other with the captive pandas, and, in the scrum of reporters, one journalist had found himself pushed up against the bars of a panda's cage. In next to no time, the occupant had bitten a chunk out of the man's backside.

Bamboo is mighty tough stuff, so jaws capable of crushing something that hard can munch their way through most things. A human backside, even a seasoned journalist's, must be tender compared with bamboo. The journalist was lucky: when the animals at Wo Long are given a leg of pork as a treat, they usually deal with it wholesale, chewing up meat, gristle, bones and everything.

Any such thoughts were far from my mind as I filmed Qian-Qian. It was a lovely autumn day. I was in China, I was filming a panda and it was all going rather well. A shout from behind me pricked my smug bubble. Ken translated, 'They have run out of sugar cane.'

'Can they get some more?'

'No time. Look, she is coming.'

I turned round and indeed Qian-Qian was bumbling along the track towards me. She looked great so I swung the camera round to get the shot. Down the viewfinder she was filling frame so I started filming her, and as I did so a strange thing happened. It has happened to me since, but this was my first experience of what I can only call 'camera courage'. To my mind Qian-Qian stopped being a real live animal and became just an image down the viewfinder. My brain lost the idea that outside my viewfinder a large and rather fierce animal was coming straight for me.

'No. She will hurt you,' I heard Ken shout. 'We must go quick.'

He shook my arm and I looked up from my camera scowling and ready to tell him what I thought of him for spoiling my shot. As I caught sight of Qian-Qian, understanding dawned. She was a real animal, not just an image on a screen. She obviously meant business and she was moving fast. She was coming to get me.

I was all thumbs as I fumbled to unhitch the camera from the tripod. (There was no way I was going to leave my precious camera for a ravening beast to maul.) I tried to scramble up the slope only to fall flat on my face. (The camera was safely in the air, of course.) Ken grabbed the tripod and made a better job of escape than me. I set off again, but through my panic I heard a soft noise, a popping fizz, somewhere behind me. I got up again and kept on scrambling, but general laughter broke out behind me as Ken came back to help me.

'It's OK,' said Ken. 'She's gone over there. Mr. Chan called her away from you.'

I looked down the slope and all I could see of Qian-Qian was her backside heading away from us. It was not much of a shot, but it was a huge relief.

'Qian-Qian has learned to chase cameramen,' Ken went on. 'If Mr. Chan stops giving her sugar cane, she goes straight for the cameraman.'

'How many cameramen have filmed her here?' I asked.

'Oh maybe fifty.'

'And how many has she managed to attack?'

'Quite a few of them.'

Suddenly the disadvantages of using captive animals were brought home to me. Pandas may be on the verge of extinction, but they are certainly not stupid animals. Every time Qian-Qian chases or attacks a cameraman, her assembled keepers lure her away from her intended victim with tasty tit-bits and special goodies. What more encouragement could a girl ask for? Chasing cameramen brings her extra food, so chasing cameramen has become a regular part of her repertoire. And I was relieved to say that yet again it had worked. Mr Chan had distracted Qian-Qian with something tasty.

I sat down again, and looked around. Below me there was an amazing sight. All four of the keepers were standing round in a gleeful group. In the middle of the group was Mr. Chan holding a can. At the other end of the can was one of the rarest animals in the world, the symbol of conservation, and she was drinking from the can. I might not approve of the way they were turning this splendid animal into a circus act, but it was a huge relief all the same. The soft fizzing sound I had heard was the ring-pull on the can being opened, and even if I had failed to identify the sound, Qian-Qian knew better: it had stopped her in her tracks. There is one thing Qian-Qian likes even more than sugar cane or a fresh leg of cameraman, and that is beer.

CHAPTER FOURTEEN

I Know a Hawk from a Handsaw

I REMEMBER AS A BOY BEING told how to identify a sparrow hawk. If you saw a grey/brown blur followed by a terrific commotion from the birds all around, then you had probably just seen one. If only I had remembered this before I tried to make a film about sparrow hawks, I might have avoided the near hopeless endeavour it turned out to be. However, it had one good spin-off. I was introduced to the joys of filming a falconer's bird, and I learned that a trained bird of prey can be a gift to a cameraman.

The thing about a falconer's bird though is that it arrives complete with falconer, and the three-way relationship between cameraman, falconer and bird can be a rather tense one. The friction stems from our different hopes. I want to film a bird that looks just like a wild one, but behaves more predictably and more controllably. The falconer wants to be sure he still has a bird to take home with him when we finish filming. The bird wants something to eat.

By the time the falconer arrives, he or she will have spent many hours over many days and months looking after and training the bird, so losing it is a hideous worry that looms over his shoulder all the time. As a result, a falconer's bird usually arrives at the filming location fully equipped with a tiny radio homing device strapped to its leg, or sewn onto a tail feather, with the aerial wire trailing out behind the bird as it flies.

'It'll have to come off,' I say.

'No way. You can hardly see it, and I'm not flying her without her radio.' Impasse.

This is not the way to approach the problem. Over the years I have learned to open the debate rather more gently, and I have worked out that the best approach is to imagine I am meeting a new mother with her tiny baby. In both situations, the first thing that is called for is a great deal of clucking and cooing. Even after that, some of the important questions have a familiar ring to them, so my side of the conversation tends to go much as follows.

'Isn't she beautiful. What's her name?'

As with a human baby, it's important to get the gender right, but if in doubt, with a falconer's bird at least, female is the one to bet on. This is a safer bet than trying to guess the gender of human babies from the colour of their clothes, and the reason is that most falconers fly female birds. This is because in almost all birds of prey, the female is quite a bit bigger than the male, and this makes her easier to work with.

'How old is she?'

With humans, I use this in an attempt to cover my inability to judge the age of babies, but with falconers it serves a different purpose. The vast majority of falconers' birds are captive bred these days, so they are handled from fledging. Any bird that is more than a year old has probably been flown for quite a long time, so presumably she is a good one.

'What does she weigh?'

With very young human babies I sometimes omit this because it usually precipitates an account of birth traumas, but with older babies it is very useful. With falconers it is an even more crucial question. Falconers train their birds to come for food, and a bird will only fly reliably if she is a bit hungry. In falconry parlance, a bird is 'sharp' or 'keen' when she is at her flying weight, which is just a bit below her maintenance weight. So by asking how heavy a bird is, I usually elicit an answer that tells me what margin we have between the bird being sharp and being fully fed.

'How did you get hold of her?'

This is a slightly unusual question to ask a new mother, but gives a falconer the chance to explain the beginnings of his relationship with the bird. That relationship is an intimate one, and you must approach warily. Perhaps it's best to think of it as an adoption rather than a birth, but the parent model is certainly the one to work from. It also acts as a reminder of that old theatrical warning: never work with children or animals. Filming a falconer's bird totally flies in the face of this advice. You are working with an animal, an honorary child and an adoptive parent. Tread carefully.

'She is very advanced for her age.'

If I hear myself saying this to a falconer, I know I have got a bit carried away with my analogy.

'What does she eat now?'

This is safer ground, and human mothers always feel obliged to answer this question very fully. With a falconer it opens up a whole new area of necessary concern. Wild birds of prey spend their lives chasing their food, and tearing apart tough meals. Birds' beaks grow constantly, but wild birds of prey wear their beaks down by tackling their bone-filled diet. Falconers generally give their birds day old chicks from chicken hatcheries, so their diet may be reasonably balanced, but their meals are soft and pappy compared with the real thing. As a result, a falconer has to trim his bird's beak to keep it in shape: an untrimmed beak looks very unnatural so it becomes an early subject of conversation.

Once the falconer has taken the bird's hood off, I usually try to take a few shots of just the bird's head against a series of different backgrounds. These are always useful to the editor, and generally calm everybody down, because if all else fails, we at least get something from the day's efforts. But you can only delay the thorny question of the homing device for so long, and eventually it has to be broached.

'I wonder if it would be a good idea to try one or two flights with the radio on, just to see how she's behaving today?'

I have a huge respect for falconers, and I really enjoy working with them so I recognise that cutting off a radio is a tense moment. I have often thought that I would like to take up falconry myself, but every time I work with a falconer, I realise that I simply don't have the patience for it. The frustration of a bird doing something ridiculous when all you want is to get it to eat would drive me to distraction. No, I stick to filming, and leave the patience (and the decision about the radio) to the falconer.

The dilemma with the radio brings us straight back to the bird's weight. Every time the bird flies, she must receive a small amount of food as a reward for returning to the fist. She has learned to fly to the falconer for food and food is the basis of their relationship. Most falconers recognise this and avoid any thought of the bird having a dog-like devotion to its handler. It is nothing but cupboard love, and a bird will only fly reliably if it is sharp. Once it has had enough to eat, even a well-trained bird is liable to fly off. Then, suddenly everybody wishes that the tracking radio was still attached.

Giving the bird a morsel of food after each flight means that there is a strict limit to the number of flights she can do before the edge comes off her hunger, and she starts to misbehave. The smaller the bird the smaller this margin of safety, so with something like a sparrow hawk or a kestrel, the falconer only has a range of about forty grams to play with, and that is not much. Forty grams is the difference between watching the bird fly off and seeing her collapse from hunger. This translates into a grand total of only about ten or fifteen flights.

With a big bird of prey, things are much easier, so I got very excited when I was asked to film a Chilean black-chested buzzard eagle named Ella. She was slightly smaller than a golden eagle I had worked with some years before, but still very impressive. She was fully seventy-five centimetres from her head to the tip of her tail, and must have weighed several kilos, so she was quite a weight to have on your fist. Ella was hit by a bus as a young bird, and despite her size a bus was more than she could manage. As a result, she had spent almost her entire life at a 'rescue centre'. There she lived in a reasonable size cage till a man called Christian Gonzales borrowed her and trained her up for me to film.

The three of us, Ella, Christian and I tackled our first, unexpected, hurdle when we had to drive through Santiago, the Chilean capital, with Ella on the back seat of Christian's beat-up estate car. For the first time in my life I had some inkling of what it must feel like to chauffeur royalty. Everywhere we went, people were laughing and pointing at us: some even waved. When we stopped at traffic lights, pedestrians swarmed round us and very reasonably asked what was going on. The crowd on one side of the car heard Christian explain that we were making a programme for television about the wildlife of Chile. On my side, in halting Spanish, I managed to say that her name was Ella and that she was a bird. A foreigner who spoke no Spanish driving around with an eagle in the car was even funnier than just a bird in a car, so we left a trail of hilarity behind us. The object of all this interest was totally unconcerned, but then she had her hood on, and could see none of the commotion she left in her wake.

When we reached our filming location, Ella showed her star quality. Christian could put her up onto any perch I chose, and she would sit there looking lovely till I asked him to call her off. Then, at Christian's first call, she responded by flying straight to the glove. With falconers' birds, perfect behaviour means promptness, and Ella was doing wonderfully. If Christian hid his glove after he called her off, she would fly round him in great elegant circles giving me a golden opportunity to film her flying free. We were doing well. It was time for the hunting sequence.

We had already filmed a wild bird circling and plummeting to earth to take its prey, now we wanted to film the close shots to cut in with the wild material. So Christian put Ella onto a suitable tree. I put the camera on the ground, and asked Christian to put his glove, with some food in it, just below the camera lens. The idea was that Ella would fly straight towards me and then, at the last moment, she would swing her talons forward and land virtually on the lens. I was after the prey's view of its impending doom.

Ella came off her perch straight towards me, and she looked perfect, menacing and deadly with her wings and tail working busily while her head was locked, gazing fixedly at the camera. About two metres short of the camera, she suddenly landed and walked the last bit. My dashing killer had turned into an ugly duckling at the crucial moment.

We tried again, but this time we had the camera a bit farther from the food. Still the short walk took all the drama out of the shot. We tried just having food on the ground without the glove, and she still insisted on walking the last little bit. We tried having the food plus camera at the edge of a small rock, so that there was a steep little drop from me to the ground. She flew towards me, landed on the ground and then ingloriously tried to scrabble up to the food only to end up stranded pathetically at the bottom of the rock.

She would fly happily to the glove when Christian held it up, but we needed her landing on the ground because the chief food of black-chested buzzard eagles is a little ground dwelling rodent called a degu. We had already filmed degus, so now we needed Ella to come down to the ground and look as though she was taking a degu. But nothing would persuade her to land on the glove or her food if they were on the ground. The glove held up in the air – fine, down on the ground – no way. It seemed a small distinction to me, but evidently there was a world of difference to Ella. We tried everything, and Ella defeated us hands down.

Eventually, we decided to try a different tack. I wanted as much drama as possible, and we worked out that it would be best if Ella could drop suddenly into shot looking towards the camera. So I put on a spare glove, and we transferred Ella to my fist. Christian stood in front of her and, gently taking hold of her entire body, he lifted her off the glove. Birds take a dim view of being held this way, and a bird as big as Ella can make her opinion felt, so she screamed and scrabbled frantically. A screaming, kicking eagle is not to be underestimated. Her legs were pumping like pistons and with her talons spread, she was a formidable sight. Eventually she settled down, and Christian felt he had her safely.

I went back to kneeling with the camera on the ground, and Christian stood over me holding Ella just above my field of view. I turned the camera on, and gave Christian the word. He dropped Ella onto the agreed spot just in front of the camera, and she landed with talons splayed and wings raised. She gathered herself together and stood exactly where I wanted her, looking not just noble but positively imperial.

We had our shot, but Christian and I were both still intrigued to know why Ella refused to fly to food put on the ground. Obviously, with her strange hang-up, there was no way she could survive in the wild, so we had to take her back to the rescue centre when we had finished filming, and this gave us a chance to find out why she behaved in this odd way. The answer was predictably simple.

Evidently, when Ella first arrived, she attacked her keeper a couple of times, so they had to devise a way to feed her safely. A small box was added to the side of the cage, and her food was always put in the box. As a result, the only way Ella could approach her food was by walking to it, and reaching into the little box to hook it out. This had become such an ingrained habit that she refused to approach food on the ground in any other way. It was a sad fate for such a handsome bird.

Even if you manage to navigate the rocky waters of the triangular relationship between cameraman, falconer and bird, there always seem to be residual problems with trained animals. You never quite know what baggage the animal brings along with her. A falconer's bird, in fact any captive animal, can be a gift to a cameraman, but the Trojan horse was a gift, and look what hidden baggage it held, and what it did for the Trojans.

CHAPTER FIFTEEN

Cold Comfort

IN MAY 1881 CAPTAIN BENJAMIN LEIGH SMITH sailed from Peterhead in Northeast Scotland in his ship *Eira*. On board were twenty-five men including the crew, and they sailed north-east till they reached the Norwegian coast near Bergen. They followed the coast on the same heading, till they reached first the Arctic Circle and then the North Cape. From there they still headed north because Benjamin Leigh Smith wanted to reach the North Pole.

A hundred years later I was offered an opportunity to follow much the same journey and I jumped at it. It was one of those trips I had always longed to make and it gave me my first opportunity to get up to the Arctic. We set sail from Kiel in North Germany. We too sailed up along the Norwegian coast, crossing the Arctic Circle. We never saw the North Cape because it was shrouded in mist, and we were heading for Franz Joseph Land, hundreds of kilometres north of the North Cape. There I again picked up the trail of Leigh Smith since this was where he and his frustrated expedition spent most of their time because their passage north was blocked by ice.

This collection of islands was just about the last place on earth to be discovered. An Austrian expedition bumped into the archipelago in 1873 as their ship drifted helpless in the polar ice, and they named it after their glorious emperor. Like Leigh Smith eight years later, they were trying to reach the North Pole: it was very much the thing for explorers to do during the last decades of the nineteenth century.

We sailed in a Russian research ship, and joined up with one of the huge Russian nuclear powered icebreakers for the final part of the journey through the ice to Franz Joseph Land. We were to see quite a bit of these astounding vessels on our trip; the height of a tower block, they can smash their way through ice a metre thick at more than fifteen knots. The bows are reinforced with over a metre of steel, and the nuclear plant produces enough power to run a good size city. As a final bizarre twist to all this, I learned that these titans were no longer employed to keep the north coast of Russia open for shipping as they had in the Soviet days, they were chartered by an American tour company to take affluent tourists to the North Pole. Their schedule brought an icebreaker past our camp every three weeks or so.

Unlike the icebreakers, Leigh Smith's ship the *Eira* was not specially built for the Arctic conditions, so he had her modified before he left. Her wooden bow was strengthened with oak to make it several inches thick, and she carried a steam engine that developed fifty horsepower. He wrote that this engine was to 'power them through the sea ice'. Fifty horsepower is less than most family cars today, and this huge discrepancy in technology started to give me some appreciation of the conditions under which Leigh Smith reached Franz Joseph Land a hundred years before us.

When we arrived I could only echo Scott's comment about the South Pole: 'Great God! This is an awful place.'

I had come to a monochrome world. The sky was grey. The land was a sheet of off-white snow with black rocks stabbing through it. The sea was ice: not flat but agonisingly contorted into smashed cliffs and jagged pinnacles. There was nothing restful to be seen.

It took some time for me to see the beauty of the Arctic, but when I did, I fell in love with it. The shapes of the landscape are wonderfully clear because they're not clothed in vegetation. The sea ice is constantly moving, producing a landscape that is forever changing. And when the sun breaks through the whole place is transformed into fairyland. The ice stops being dirty white and shines blue and green. What vegetation there is changes to vivid emerald, and the melting snow produces small streams rimmed with bright red moss, completing the rainbow. The sun is always low in the sky giving glorious shadows and texture to the landscape, and the animals are so numerous that they come to dominate the scene. The birds, the wind and the incessant creaking and groaning of the sea ice provide the only sounds to be heard.

I was part of a huge group of over forty members, organised by Austrian television. We were there to celebrate the original Austrian expedition that had discovered the islands and to make a whole series of television programmes about the place, and its original Austrian discovery. This last involved the absolute star of the show – a full size replica of the ship that first reached the islands. She was a three-mast schooner named *Tegettoff*, and her twentieth-century replica travelled north with us, ingloriously packed into twelve containers on the deck of the research ship from Kiel. With her came a crew of a dozen or so stagehands who were to re-create this ghost ship near to where the original had sunk.

The set building crew was put ashore on a small spit of land named Ziegler Island because there was a suitable spot for them to build the *Tegettoff*. They and their twelve containers were dumped on the ice beside our ship, and as a final touch, a big red tractor was deposited beside the containers. This was to be their source of power, and as we left, the stage crew set about using it to drag their containers to the gravel bank where they intended to build the replica ship.

That left the four camera crews including my assistant Philip and myself, and we all sailed off to another island to establish our own camp. Philip and I were the only English

Gibbons float through the trees defying gravity, and at dawn established pairs sing a beautiful love duet. (*photo Jane-Marie Franklin*)

BELOW Watching a mountain gorilla was like looking into a distorting mirror at the fair: the similarities made it obvious that we were related, but the differences were fascinating. (*photo Ian Redmon*)

My preparation for filming an egyptian vulture involved squirting the contents of thirty hens' eggs into a souvenir ostrich egg. (*photo James Gray*)

BELOW I prefer not to film captive animals, but it would have taken months of effort and unbelievable luck to get even one shot like this of a wild panda. So I filmed Qian-Qian in the enclosure at the breeding centre in Wo-Long with the mountains of Szechwan in the background. (*photo James Gray*)

ABOVE Walruses are
lovely creatures but they
must have the most evil
smelling breath in the
animal kingdom.
(*photo Philip Lovel*)

The cliffs in Franz
Joseph Land were
high, steep and made of
horrible soft crumbling
rock. When Philip and
I roped both the camera
and ourselves to the
cliff, we got hopelessly
tangled, so I ended up
just tying the camera on.
(*photo James Gray*)

The replica of the *Tegettoff* that our expedition built in Franz Joseph Land became a looming ghostly presence on the ice. (*photo Philip Lovel*)

About a minute after our tractor fell through the ice, Peter the driver surfaced spluttering and terrified but alive. It then took us thirty-six hours to salvage the tractor using winches, scaffolding and ropes. (*photo James Gray*)

When I managed to film golden monkeys in the foothills of the Himalayas, shining like Christmas decorations on the pine trees, I realised I was looking at one of the most precious animals I would ever see. (*photo Heather Angel*)

ABOVE The morning after we filmed the golden monkeys in China, Chris emerged from our tent rather slowly, nursing a serious hangover. (*photo James Gray*)

This rare picture shows me filming out of a helicopter and not being sick; however, minutes later I reverted to form, much to the disgust of the rest of the crew. (*photo James Gray*)

ABOVE There are some
eighty species of chameleon
in Madagascar, and
fortunately most of the
island people see them as
dangerous spirits and leave
them severely alone.
(*photo Chris Catton*)

In southern Madagascar a
carved bull's head topping
a totem pole on a grave
proclaims the wealth of
the deceased.
(*photo Chris Catton*)

This elephant in Thailand looked so placid that I couldn't resist getting closer and closer to him. It was only later that I learned about his homicidal past. (*photo Jane-Marie Franklin*)

BELOW Singing, dancing and daylong festivities marked the funeral we filmed in southern Madagascar. About a dozen bullocks were butchered that day, and at least forty litres of rum were drunk. (*photo Philip Lovel*)

people on the expedition and had responsibility for filming the wildlife. I had the added private agenda of wanting to find out more about Leigh Smith.

My interest in Leigh Smith and his expedition received a great boost when the research ship deposited us all on Cap Flora, virtually the most south-westerly part of the archipelago. We were to camp there for our first six or seven weeks, and this was excellent news because it was exactly where Leigh Smith and his party had spent much of their time mapping the archipelago.

Our first filming task was on our doorstep at Cap Flora. As we arrived, I noticed a pair of Arctic skuas flying around in a very possessive sort of way. They are extremely dramatic birds that parasite gulls by chasing them till they regurgitate any food they are carrying. It was the first time I had seen them properly, and they were spectacular. Their flight is an object lesson in restrained power until they see a gull carrying food. Then the skua changes gear and sets off at such speed that it is suddenly metamorphosed into a hunting peregrine or a fighter plane. The ensuing dog-fight may last for several minutes, but there is never any doubt that the skua will win. A gull and a skua are about the same size, so to a boxing promoter it might sound like a fair match up, but the contest is rather like that between a rat and a terrier, it can only end one way. To begin with, the skua chases the gull, relentlessly zig-zagging across the sky till it catches its victim. Then it usually grabs a wing or the tail and literally shakes the gull out of the sky. Eventually the gull coughs up its food and the skua lets go of the gull to catch its regurgitated meal in mid-air. Skuas are aggression made flesh, and they put on the most breathtaking aerobatics displays, so I just had to film them.

They obviously had a nest nearby, and we quite quickly worked out roughly where it was. Philip found some posts and a roll of tape, and we strung together a makeshift fence around the skua nest area. That evening at supper, I spoke to the assembled company in my best, broken German and asked everybody to keep outside our fence. I explained that we were going to film the birds as soon as possible, and they needed protection in the mean time. Anyway, I hope that was what I said. In hindsight, I think I might have got the word 'skua' confused, in which case I probably spoke at some length about the breeding behaviour of little pointed bits of metal.

When at last we finished moving all the most vital equipment from the ship to our campsite, Philip and I turned our attention to filming the skuas, and I soon learned how vital our fence was. As I ducked under the tape, a screaming bird materialised from nowhere and hurled itself straight at me.

'Achtung! Stuka!' shouted Philip. It took me half a second to realise this was no mere slip of the tongue on Philip's part. It was frighteningly accurate, but hardly tactful, given the company we were in.

The skua turned, banked and launched a second assault while Philip made machine-gun noises. After three or four attacks, the bird flew back towards its nest, but we had clearly worried it. That's good, I told myself, they're still nesting despite all the comings and goings. It will obviously give me another distraction display if I go any closer.

The first bird hit me fair and square landing a powerful peck from its vicious hooked beak on the top of my head. First blood to the skuas. Philip was convulsed with laughter. I backed off a bit, but that was wrong again. The birds clearly took appeasement as a sign of weakness, so now both skuas joined in the attack. They came at me in waves, one after the other screaming and pecking at my head. Flailing my arms like a demented windmill I retreated farther and farther away from my tormentors till I was virtually back at camp.

From that moment on, the skuas extended their territory and undertook with missionary zeal to harass everybody who came near them. They obviously wanted to clear the entire Arctic of film crews. They became braver and more belligerent till one day a helicopter from the icebreaker flew in to bring us some supplies, and the skuas attacked the helicopter. They both flew straight at it, only to be blasted out of the sky by the downdraft from the rotor. It was the only time I saw them defeated.

By now everybody realised that our fence had suffered a total role reversal: it was protecting humans from the skuas. Almost more importantly, it served as a crowd barrier for the audience we attracted every time Philip and I tried to film the birds. Eventually we succeeded, but, to the disappointment of the crowd, I had to do it from a hide. Normally I use a hide to avoid frightening the birds but, like the fence, the hide had also experienced a role reversal.

As we worked on the skuas, Philip realised that we, the wildlife team, had developed a new role in the expedition. Our antics had become the prime source of entertainment, and that seemed like a good niche to occupy. As the only two Brits, we were in a tiny minority, so Philip decided that we should take on the role of expedition comedians. What he really meant was that he would become expedition comedian, and I would become his stooge, his straight man and the butt of half his jokes. My one proviso was that I felt it would be a good idea for Philip to steer clear of his Spitfire pilot impressions. So that was the deal, and we agreed that from then on we would film the wildlife and try to keep the rest of the party amused.

After the skuas, it was time to film the flowers.

'No way,' said Philip. 'We're never going to raise any laughs with flowers.' But I decided we had to go ahead anyway.

There are only about thirty species of plant on the islands, and most of them seemed to be living on Cap Flora so whole areas of the peninsula resembled a glorious rockery. The best to film were the ones that form cushions, purple saxifrage and the pinker moss campion because they provided compact masses of intense colour. Next came the Arctic poppies, which have creamy flowers that stick up about ten centimetres above the surface of the scree. Like satellite stations, they track the sun across the sky, and apparently this keeps the centre of the flower several degrees above air temperature.

Philip and I were talking about this when Philip raised an interesting point in his inimitable way.

'That's got to be crap,' he said. 'They'd tie themselves in knots if they really followed the sun. Or maybe they'd twist their own heads off.'

Philip had a point and I'd love to know the answer. We were only a few hundred kilometres from the North Pole, and it was mid-summer, so there was no night. If the poppies really did follow the sun, the flowers would have to rotate through 360 degrees every sunny day.

Whatever the poppies' problems, the business of twenty-four-hour daylight became a real problem for us humans, especially when it came to sleeping. It just felt wrong to crawl into my tent and snuggle down in my sleeping bag while the sun was shining. I thought longingly of the airline blackout masks I'd left at home.

The twenty-four-hour daylight had a hundred thousand allies in preventing sleep. The cliffs behind our campsite were smothered in nesting birds, and they made an incessant noise. Even the cliffs themselves joined in the racket because they showered down rock falls as the ice thawed in the spring sunshine. I came to use earplugs when I crawled into my sleeping bag, and felt incredibly stupid for doing so, but it helped.

The crumbling cliffs and the birds nesting on them had to be the next thing that Philip and I turned our attention to. The density of birds in these colonies is truly amazing. They start to arrive from the south during May, when winter has finally passed, and the sea ice has broken up. By the end of the month flocks of tens of thousands appear and birds swarm around the cliffs. By mid-June, when we arrived, every cliff ledge was home to a pair of guillemots or kittewakes, so we started work on them.

The first thing we found was that not every cliff ledge was home to nesting birds: they only chose the inaccessible ledges so we spent ages trying to find nests that we could reach. When eventually we found a gully that took us up to a few nests, we could appreciate those birds close up, and they are magnificent. The guillemots are lovely clean-cut birds, black above and white below with a thin white line through the eye like rather overdone makeup. Kittewakes are smallish gulls with pure black wing tips and yellowish bills that are rather delicate by comparison with most other gulls.

The disadvantage with appreciating these birds close up was the overpowering stink of guano and dead fish. Everything we touched was covered in muck, however, after a while we became used to the smell. What that actually meant was that we had started to blend in with our surroundings and we smelt as bad as the birds. That evening at supper, Philip and I had no trouble finding a space to sit, in fact we had a whole table to ourselves. Fortunately the man in charge of running the camp took it as a strong hint that it was time he rigged up some showers, so everybody thanked us in the long run. It was just as well because we spent the better part of two weeks filming up by the cliffs, and being shunned for that long would have become a bit demoralising.

Every fine day, Philip and I headed up to the bird colony and our chosen spot where we had picked out a pair of kittewakes about a metre and a half away. They were just completing their nest building and courtship, so there was still a huge amount of activity from them. Kittewakes specialise in nesting on tiny ledges, and their courtship behaviour has evolved to match their chosen, rather cramped, nest sites. They make none of the flamboyant gestures or movements of other gulls. Kittewakes go in for minimalist courtship, with small head movements that give precise signals to each other, but since we were so close to the nearest pair, they were great to film. On the other side of our scree-filled gully there were guillemots sitting on their eggs. They don't make a nest at all, but their eggs are so pointed that, when they are knocked, they roll in a tight circle and hardly ever fall off the ledge. This was just as well, because there was a terrific amount of jostling on the ledges as birds came and went.

Arctic birds always strike me as particularly beautiful. Their markings are unusually precise so they look immaculate and well groomed. These are hardly qualities that I aspire to myself, but I admire them in others, so I loved filming the cliff birds: they flatter the camera, or vice versa. The background helped too because, behind our featured nests, a curtain of vertical cliffs stretched as far as the eye could see. These cliffs were plastered with birds sitting on their nests and the air was heavy with birds flying to and from the cliffs. This spectacle was perfectly set off by the ice filled sea and the deep blue sky. At least that was what it looked like on good days, and we only went up to the bird cliffs on good days.

Among the boulders at the foot of the cliffs there were huge numbers of little auks nesting, and I developed a love/hate relationship with these birds. They are a smaller version of the guillemots that we had filmed on the cliffs, also black above and white below but with stubby little bills and no neck with the result that they look very compact and rather vulnerable. The members of each pair take it in turns to sit on the eggs, so there were always thousands of sitting birds invisible beneath the boulders. The ones that were taking time out sat around on top of the rocks in little knots like teenagers with nothing to do. Almost all the birds in the Arctic are very easily approached, and little auks were no exception, so with patience we managed to watch and film them from a couple of metres or so, and they were enchanting.

However at the sight of their chief predator, a glaucous gull, all the little auks that had nothing better to do took off in flocks of thousands to wheel round in circles screaming at the intruder till eventually he left, and they landed back at their take off rock. Glaucous gulls came past every few minutes, so the little auks made an important contribution to the 'Keep James Awake Campaign'.

My attitude to these little birds developed an extra twist when one day we spotted a polar bear with her year-old cub among the colony. So we grabbed the camera, and slowly got close enough to film what was going on. What we saw was the mother ploughing her way through the colony, and heaving aside boulders as if they had been stage props made of polystyrene. It was the first indication I had of the phenomenal strength of these beautiful animals. As she turned each boulder over, both she and her cub grabbed the incubating birds that scuttled off to escape the disturbance. Above the bears' heads there was a swarm of screaming birds just flying round and round impotently. The bears were catching birds left and right, and stuffing them into their mouths, feathers and all. They had blood all over them, and were spitting out feathers as they lunged to catch more disturbed birds.

Little auks are about the same size as blackbirds, so each one could have been no more than a taste for a bear, but the colony was huge, and an endless supply of canapés can make a meal. They were totally engrossed in their banquet, so Philip and I managed to get quite close to them, and filmed them through the blizzard of birds around their heads. After an hour or so the diners wandered off to a grassy patch, where they lay down and fell asleep in the sun, leaving behind them a trail of death, destruction and over-turned rocks.

From the bird cliffs, we could see not only the bears' trail through the little auk colony, but also the tracks that we humans had left on the land. All around the campsite our paths cut dark lines in the tundra. From a distance, we could see that we were marking the place and marring its beauty even as we tried to film and record that beauty. But it wasn't only us. One day, when Philip and I were working on the bird cliffs, one of the icebreakers came to Cap Flora, and we watched as thirty or so visitors were flown ashore by helicopter. From the landing site, their paths fanned out like the spokes of a wheel as they explored the area. In itself this sounds unremarkable: but we could still see those paths weeks later when eventually we left. The Arctic is so fragile that paths made by just a few feet remain for months and even years. A tiny number of tourists or film crews on these islands could destroy their ecology and beauty forever.

This became painfully clear when we found the remains of a really old path leading up from the sea. It was partly covered in moss and lichen, but it was obvious that somebody had shifted the boulders to make a convenient path. It was some time before I realised what it was. Over a hundred years before our visit, Leigh Smith and his crew must have made this path when they had to shift their few stores inland from the shore on 21 August 1881, the day that their ship *Eira* sank at Cap Flora.

Nearby we found the remains of their shelter. With typically English humour they named it 'Flora Cottage' but it was pitifully small, about four metres wide and twelve metres long. They had constructed it when they realised they were stuck on Cap Flora for the winter. They used the only materials available to them – rocks for the walls and moss to fill the gaps in an attempt to keep out the polar wind. I had read about this before I left England, so standing beside the remains of 'Flora Cottage' was an eerie experience. I could see that it was divided into three sections, just as it said in the account that I had read. Evidently the centre portion was the kitchen and eating area. At one end was a dormitory for the twenty men. The room at the other end was for Leigh Smith and the four officers. True, the area for the twenty men was a bit bigger than the officers' portion, but it was clear that even in adversity these people stuck to their social distinctions.

It was just as they prepared to leave for home that Leigh Smith's expedition developed all the makings of a classic tragedy. They had failed to get further north than Franz Joseph Land because of the ice, but, as a consolation for failing to reach the pole, they devoted themselves to exploring, mapping and naming the islands. In late August, winter starts to regain its hold on the land so they prepared to sail south. They had loaded almost all the stores on board, when the lookout spotted an iceberg bearing down on them. The wind had dropped so they couldn't sail to safety, and they didn't have time to steam up their little engine. Half an hour after it was spotted, the iceberg crushed the *Eira* against the shore ice, and she sank.

During that half-hour, the men worked feverishly to unload stores, and managed to salvage a fair amount. This included the stove, some of the coal and some food. The *Eira*'s whalers (open rowing boats about five metres long) had been taken away from the iceberg's impact, and most importantly they had collected the rifles and ammunition. With this they had to face an Arctic winter, and an Arctic winter isn't something to take lightly. For one thing the cold is intense. On top of that, winter lasts for the better part of eight months, and to make it even more daunting, the sun sets in October and doesn't rise again till February. So they had half an hour to prepare themselves for eight months of cold and dark with nowhere to live and not much to eat.

Fortunately they had earlier deposited some stores in a cabin on one of the other islands for their intended return the following year, and they managed to recover this a couple of months after *Eira* sank. Their plight was also improved by the fact that they managed to rescue some drink. They had to face the arctic winter with just 320 litres of rum, 36 bottles of champagne, 60 bottles of beer, 12 bottles of gin, 18 bottles of whisky and some sherry.

The amazing thing is that they all survived. Alcohol poisoning must have been high on the list of dangers, along with the cold, starvation, scurvy and boredom. They lived through the winter in their little shelter eating what they shot: thirty-four polar bears and twenty-four walrus. Then in June of the following year, when the ice broke up a bit, they pushed their little whalers across the sea ice and rowed across patches of open water south to an island off the north coast of Russia called Novia Zemlia. This journey took them forty-three days, but it was worth it because the day after they reached Novia Zemlia they were picked up by a rescue party sent out from London.

Knowledge of this remarkable story added a frisson to the time I spent at Cap Flora because I had read about the Leigh Smith expedition when I visited the Scott Polar Institute in Cambridge a month or so before I left England. What I had read was humbling even as I read it, but standing next to the remains of 'Flora Cottage' really brought it home to me. The endurance of those men totally over-

shadowed our efforts. The Arctic is a tough place to do anything, and they had survived right through a winter.

We were finding it hard work just moving about on the
thawing tundra carrying cameras, lenses and so on in summer. The rocks crumbled as we trod on them, scree slid
away under our feet as we tried to climb it and the flat areas
were peaty, wet and full of holes, so we were for ever stum-
bling and falling over.

Cap Flora was wonderful for the plants and the sea
birds, but there were relatively few other animals for us to
film there. Bears only came past occasionally and there
were virtually no Arctic foxes. There were a few seals but
we never managed to get near them. However, as our time
there went on we saw more and more walruses. I had done
my homework and read up about walruses before I left
England, but that hadn't prepared me for the real thing.
Walruses are big, and with their tusks and the bristles
round their mouths they have a wonderful hang dog
appearance, beautifully captured in the *Alice in Wonderland*
illustrations. Like Lewis Carroll's walrus, real ones eat
shellfish though I doubt they often come across oysters.
They feed by using their tusks to stir up the mud, and then
they use their bristles to find the animals in the mud.
Having found a clam, a walrus deals with it in a unique way.
It holds the shell in its jaws, and draws its tongue backwards. This works like a hydraulic cylinder and creates
such a strong suction that the contents are pulled out of the
shell, and swallowed.

Philip summarised this fascinating bit of biology with

the comment that 'A good snog with a walrus would really tug at your heartstrings.'

We had been working at Cap Flora for about five weeks before I met a walrus properly, and it was unforgettable. We were in one of the inflatable boats we used to get about when I spotted a dozen or so on an ice flow near the land, so we stopped and watched. The walruses dived, and I imagined that was the last we were going to see of them. But they surfaced again, much closer to our little boat, and there was no doubt they were watching us as closely as we were watching them. They dived again, and we just waited.

Suddenly the water round our little inflatable erupted as ten tons of walrus rose out of the water all around us. Their heads were on a level with ours and only a metre or so away. Their tusks were pointed directly and menacingly at the flimsy plastic that was keeping us afloat. Their eyes were huge and hideously blood-shot. Their breath steamed in the cold air, and it was so rank I was afraid we might die of asphyxia. After a few minutes breathing that foetid air, my only fear was that we wouldn't die quickly enough.

Our walruses seemed to be jostling for the honour of sinking our flimsy boat, and there was absolutely nothing we could do about it. I clutched the rifle tightly, but I couldn't think of anything useful to do with it. Even Philip's supply of snappy banter ran out when confronted by all that evil smelling blubber, so we watched them in stupefied silence. Eventually, they must have decided that sucking our guts out would be rather messy, and to our great relief they swam off. We could breathe again – or we could once the smell had cleared.

'Well, we showed them didn't we?' said Philip once we'd calmed down. 'And I thought oysters were meant to be an aphrodisiac. I'm not going to touch another one if eating them makes your breath smell that bad.'

If meeting walruses was exciting, filming them was also fun. The problem was getting the camera stable. In the boat, we could usually get quite close to groups lying about on odd ice-floes, but filming them from the boat was hopeless because it was rocking about on the water. If I got onto the ice with a group of animals, they all dived off into the water, leaving me with nothing but the smell.

Eventually we solved the problem when we found an ice-floe with a dozen or so animals on it. A couple of hundred metres away was another decent bit of ice, and I set myself up on that. Then by running the boat into the back of my ice-floe, Philip used the outboard motor to move himself, me, the boat and our lump of ice towards the walruses. It took over half an hour to shift what I calculated to be well over fifty tons of ice, but slowly we closed in on our quarry. And they just didn't care. Obviously, bits of ice are always moving about in their world, so they hardly bothered to look up even when our ice-floe crashed into theirs.

A dozen walruses lay there scratching and sunning themselves, and they totally ignored us. Watching them from close quarters, I realised that they weren't just scratching themselves though, they were scratching each other. And they were rubbing up against each other. They were also doing a lot of stroking and grunting. In fact, there was a walrus orgy going on in front of our eyes. You can't have too much sex in a wildlife programme, so I used up quite a bit of film on those walruses.

Those walruses changed Philip's life. 'I take back what I said about not eating oysters. I'm going to feed them to all my girlfriends.'

After about six weeks at Cap Flora, the whole gang of us got on board the next passing icebreaker and headed north to join the crew who were building the *Tegettoff*. The sight that greeted us was beautiful but chilling. There, on the ice, was this elegant black ship resurrected from a hundred years ago with just one mast standing. It was the *Flying Dutchman* made real. Beside the icebreaker she was minute and so delicate that I'd have been reluctant to board her on a boating lake.

It confirmed for me my belief that those Victorian explorers must have been half-mad to venture out into this barren, menacing world. My admiration for them only increased as the weeks went on. We were equipped with the latest in cold climate gear, with breathable waterproofs, fleece inner layers, and wicking underclothes. We had no excuse for feeling cold for more than the few minutes it took to warm up clothes as we put them on.

The equipment used a hundred years earlier seemed to be based on absolutely no understanding of Arctic conditions. Leather hobnail boots might have been just the job for a gardener in Surrey, but not here. Thick woollen trousers must have become sodden as they thawed inside a tent, only to freeze solid again when the wearer went outside, losing all their insulation. The hats that people wore were designed for pheasant shooting in Norfolk, not for stopping Arctic blizzards. And yet those men survived not only summer months here, but the winters as well.

I became even more aware of these discrepancies as the summer started to fade and winter arrived. In the middle of August the wind shifted round to the North, and the temperature dropped. Ice formed again on the innumerable bits of open water and snow fell. As if to remind us of the fortitude of those earlier adventurers, the *Tegettoff* arose out of the growing ice. By now all three masts were standing up and they had sprouted rigging that was already wearing the hoarfrost that it would carry till next May.

As August progressed, and the last vestiges of summer vanished, the cold, the isolation and the bleak landscape started to tell on our whole group. Everybody became short tempered and intolerant. Rows started breaking out, and a general sense of frustration took over the party. One row became so vicious that the officer in charge of the rifles called them all in for a couple of days. We had rifles so that we could protect ourselves from bears, but he decided that the risk from bears was smaller than the risk of somebody getting shot. In an effort to distract everybody from these tensions, Philip and I looked to our role as expedition comedians, and decided we needed reinforcements. We called in *Monty Python*.

We had with us a huge battery of video equipment, and this included VHS machines with monitors. So we had all been advised to bring with us our favourite video to while away the hours when bad weather prevented us doing anything more constructive. It was a tricky decision, but I had chosen to bring with me *Monty Python and the Holy Grail*. It fitted well with the mission statement that Philip and I had dreamt up, and, much to my surprise, it rapidly became the camp favourite. Everybody watched it time and again. It became so popular that the entire expedition started quoting it in gobbets at every possible moment.

After about the third showing, Philip and I found ourselves being taken to one side and asked to explain particular words or phrases. This was almost more fun than the film itself, and I regret to say that after a while Philip embarked on a programme of disinformation. There must be several people wandering around Vienna with a rather unusual understanding of certain words. The word 'shrubbery' probably causes quite a few red faces. And as to 'The Knights who say Ni', they could never be mentioned in polite society. *Monty Python* did help to relieve some of the tensions, but it also took my feeling of unreality to new heights. The best thing is that my favourite video now gives me even more laughs than it did before I went to the Arctic.

For our last two or three weeks in Franz Joseph Land, Philip and I concentrated on filming the bears. For one thing, it kept us out of camp and the tensions that were running there. For another, Ziegler Island, where we spent the second half of our trip, was far better for bears than Cap Flora. Now we were working with them solidly and saw them most days, so we could really put some effort into getting closer to them, and learning more about them.

One of the rules for working in polar bear country is that you must carry a weapon at all times, hence the rifles. We stuck to this religiously, but when filming, it's all too easy to forget the dangers, so I decided that we would make the *Tegettoff* our base. During what we all defined as 'night', when the stage crew was sleeping, Philip and I took over the ship and night after night we used her as a safe platform to film from. It was perfect. The deck was about three metres above the level of the ice, and smoothly overhanging, so no bear could climb it. We had a cabin where we could keep vaguely warm and we set up the camera on deck ready for the bears to come and see us. For several nights we just sat and waited, and we had some success, but after a while I decided that we needed to be more proactive, and see what we could do about bringing bears to us.

It's fairly easy to attract polar bears: you simply disobey all the advice on how to behave in bear country. So we regularly put out food for them in front of our filming position. We also had a little camping gas cooker and used it alternately to cook up coffee or soup for ourselves, and to burn little bits of fat gleaned from the kitchen. The idea was to make a smell that would bring in more bears.

From the safety of the deck of the *Tegettoff* we could look out over the sea ice that stretched the ten or so kilometres to the next island. We noted almost as soon as we arrived that there was a regular movement of bears up the shore of the island opposite, so we just hoped to attract them to come over the ice and join us. The frightening thing was that our trick with the burning fat worked. Time and again we would watch through our binoculars a bear shambling along the opposite shore. Then, when it was directly down wind of us, it would turn and head straight for us. Their sense of smell is as awesomely powerful as all their other attributes.

The first time we enticed a bear to come and visit us, it was rather less than perfect. It came towards us beautifully with head lowered and huge feet swinging. Every few minutes it stopped and raised its head, sniffing before coming on. Occasionally it had to swim across a lead or crack in the ice, and then it dived in, and we would just see a head crossing the small stretch of water, till it climbed out and shook itself like a dog. Unfortunately when it reached the side of the *Tegettoff*, the bear started to behave like an animal in a zoo. It was directly below us, walking backwards and forwards, trying to get at this wonderful smell.

So Philip had a brilliant idea: he proposed that we should make a decoy seal to lure a bear into hunting behaviour. We made a framework out of wood, and covered it with a reindeer hide. Attached to one end was a fishing line that stretched the thirty or so metres to our camera position. This way we could make the decoy move a little bit just to keep any bear that arrived interested in the 'seal'. We also put a bit of rancid lard inside the decoy so that it would smell irresistible to our bear. Philip named his seal Roger.

The next three nights we tried to get Roger to attract some bears for us, but the wind was in the wrong direction, and we had no luck at all. On the fourth night the wind went round to the North again, so it turned cold, but we set up the camera, the little camping cooker and Roger. And a bear came. It came from the other side of the sound, heading straight to us. About one kilometre away it paused and looked. Philip gently pulled Roger's cord, and he moved a little. The bear sank into a new, stealthy posture, and crept towards us. When it reached a lead it slithered into the water. It swam under the next bit of ice, surfacing again much closer. At the near edge, it insinuated itself back onto the ice again, but there was no spaniel-like shaking this time, just a slow move towards Roger. It looked great, perhaps a bit far away, but I was filming it anyway.

The bear came closer and closer. Then about forty metres from Roger it stopped. It stood up to its full height and just looked at Roger. I swear that a speech bubble coming out of its mouth read, 'What the hell is that?'

It walked up to Roger and gently pushed him into the nearby water. There it set about playing with this strange new toy, ducking it and throwing it about. Fun film, but not quite what we had in mind.

It was a memorable day, both for the bear and for the date. It was 21 August: the anniversary of the sinking of the *Eira*. As if to remind us of the plight of those men, we were on the reconstructed *Tegettoff* but even so we felt vulnerable to the elements. It was fifteen degrees below zero, there was quite a wind blowing, it had started snowing, and there was that circle round a barely visible sun that tells you that it is going to go on snowing. Despite all our advanced equipment, we were decidedly uncomfortable: Leigh Smith and company must have been desperate. They were fighting for their lives: we were playing games with a polar bear. The thought of being in their boots, stuck here in these conditions was very frightening.

Our sense of isolation and the constant threat posed by the elements were crystallised by an alarming incident just before we were due to head home. It centred on the tractor that the set-building crew had to help them build the *Tegettoff*. My initial reaction to seeing a tractor in the Arctic was that it was a coarse intrusion into the pristine beauty of the place, but that was in my romantic phase just after we arrived. Later I realised how useful it was, and joined everybody else wishing that we had two or three of them. We all used it for getting about, and established a virtual road across the ice, from our camp to the *Tegettoff*.

About ten days before we were due to go home, Peter, one of the stage crew was driving out to the ship, when suddenly a huge slab of ice gave way under him, and sank. Down went the tractor with Peter still in the cab, to settle on the seabed.

Amazingly, Peter kept his head and remembered the advice given to people who drive on ice. Keep calm as the cab fills with water, and wait. At the last possible moment, take a deep breath of the remaining air, open the door and swim upwards. Then just hope that you come up through the hole in the ice. Peter did.

Very frightened and cold, Peter was pulled out of the freezing water, and rushed back to camp where he was soon dried off and warmed up. He was fine, but we were without our tractor. So the 'Save The Tractor' campaign started.

First the divers went down to locate the tractor. They found it quite quickly in about ten metres of water, so not very deep, and fortunately there was hardly any current. That lack of current had saved Peter's life because he and the tractor had gone down vertically, so he was able to come up vertically to reach the hole. The tractor lay directly below the hole.

The divers tied ropes to it, and took them up to the surface. The construction crew then had to work out how to lift the tractor with precious little in the way of mechanical help. Their normal source of power was at the bottom of the sea, so they had to improvise. It soon became like a reconstruction of the building of Stonehenge. There were A-frames and hand winches. There were pulleys attached to steel spikes driven into the ice, and cables from here to there and back again. For the final effort, everybody was assembled to add their bit of muscle hauling on one rope or another.

The recovery took about thirty-six hours, and eventually we succeeded in lifting the tractor. Slowly it emerged through the crust of ice that kept forming over the hole, till finally we had our red tractor back, sitting on the ice. Huge congratulations and a party followed.

During the night, while we were partying, the wind changed direction. The ice in the sound all broke up, and drifted out into the open ocean. Our tractor sat on one of the ice floes that drifted away, so it sailed off, cast adrift in the Arctic Ocean never to be seen again.

Philip was the only person who immediately saw the humour of the situation, but he had the good sense to keep it pretty much to himself. The divers and construction crew were aghast at the waste of their efforts, and those efforts had been huge. Everybody else saw it as yet another sign that it was high time we got out of there.

A week later, an icebreaker picked us up, and we were on our way home. Philip and I indulged in lengthy showers, huge meals and a swim in her sweltering pool. We had a sauna that was probably right on top of the nuclear pile but we really didn't care at that stage. It was so good to be in the warm.

On board I bumped into Robert Headland, the archivist at the Scott Polar Institute in Cambridge. He had helped me learn about the islands and Leigh Smith, and now he was one of the lecturers on board the ship. Chatting with him after my sauna, I told him how amazed I'd been by the sudden onset of winter, and how humbling I found accounts of the early explorers, especially their courage and resilience.

'What sort of people were they?' I asked.

'Tough,' he said. To prove his point he reminded me of the entry for 21 August in Leigh Smith's diary, which we had examined together at the institute in Cambridge. Following total disaster and facing hideous dangers, his entire diary entry for that day records its catastrophic events with two words.

'Ship Lost.'

CHAPTER SIXTEEN

There's Gold in Them There Hills

'MONKEYS HALF WAY UP THE HIMALAYAS?' I said in the tone of voice I reserve for extreme ridicule. 'You're not going to catch me out that way – not this time.'

My scorn was aimed at Chris, who has probably been my assistant more often than anybody else, and I felt he had earned a rebuke. I count Chris as a real friend, but he does have a huge capacity for making fun of me. That may be why we get on well together, but I regularly take vows not to let him catch me out again, so there was no way I was going to be taken in by his story about mountain monkeys. I know a bit about primates, so I was confident that they pretty much stick to warm places. We humans are the only ones stupid enough to venture into cold regions, and half way up the Himalayas is cold.

'No, no,' said Chris, 'there really are monkeys here.'

'So, what do they look like?'

'Well, they're quite big, with golden fur and blue faces.'

'No way. I'm not buying that one.' Even Chris had to admit that it didn't sound very convincing, but he was unshakeable. Ken our interpreter chimed in on Chris' side, and even found a book with a picture in it. He proudly showed me a photo of a cage containing a sad, vaguely yellow monkey with a strange bluish face.

Soon it wasn't only Chris and Ken, everybody was adamant that there were golden monkeys and that they lived in the mountains of Szechwan. Those mountains are the foothills of the Himalayas, and Chris and I were sharing a leaky tent on the side of one of them at the time. We were there principally to film pandas, and a few days before our discussion, a can of beer had saved me from one of those ravening monsters, so now it was time to turn our attention to the animals they share the region with, the co-stars of our programme. The producer had contacted us about the animals he thought we should film and the golden monkeys were there at number one on his list.

Soon I learned that there were two other things that everybody agreed about on the subject of golden monkeys. The first was that they were very hard to find, and the second was that the one person who just might be able to take us to see them was Lo Pen. His name kept cropping up in conversation, and he was always described as that wonderful anomaly, an ex-hunter. These people often appear when you're looking for a rare animal, but if you hope to work with the ex-hunter, it's best not to enquire too closely just when it was that he added 'ex' to his job description. This was particularly true in China, where the penalties for killing protected species are draconian. I believe that the death penalty that has been handed down for killing a panda is exceptional, but even for less precious animals, punishment may well include lengthy prison sentences.

The trouble was that Lo Pen was nowhere about, and there seemed no way of contacting him. So we struggled on with the other things we had to film, and kept gently asking about his whereabouts. Then, one day, we heard a rumour that Lo Pen had appeared, and he was prepared to meet us. So we invested in a bottle or two of liquor and went off to find him.

Lo Pen turned out to be about fifty, and truly an out-doors man. He had bright, alert eyes, weather-beaten skin and that admirable air of peace that comes from a life lived away from buildings. He was more of an observer than a lis-tener and a better listener than a talker. Even after he had drunk quite a bit of our liquor, he committed himself to very little but said he would let us know when he worked out where the monkeys were. We had to settle for that, and went back to our tent to nurse our burgeoning hangovers.

About two weeks later word reached us that Lo Pen had at last found the monkeys, and they were over the far side of the reserve. Wo Long, the reserve we were working in is huge, so this news meant that we had to pack up and shift ourselves and our equipment to another camp that would give us better access to the area the monkeys were in. Ken spoke to one of the young men in the village and he agreed to come the following day with a few of his friends to move the gear for us. They duly arrived, we paid them their fee, so they picked up our equipment cases as though they were empty and set off. Their strength and energy left us feeling big, ungainly and desperately unfit.

We followed them down the path, but to my amazement, we caught up with them round the first corner. Even as we watched, they passed their loads over to their younger sisters. It turned out that the girls were going to do the actual work once their brothers had pocketed the money. Our protests fell on deaf ears, and the discussion was cut short when the girls ran off with all our cameras on their backs. The boys smirked. We followed the girls, carrying nothing, and reached our destination a full hour after them. They had vanished, leaving us to remind each other that mountain people have larger volumes of blood and higher concentrations of red blood cells. It was the best we could come up with to console ourselves for being weaker and less fit than a bunch of schoolgirls.

That evening Lo Pen arrived in our new camp, and quietly told us that the monkeys were a few miles away, and he had seen them that day. So we had a long discussion about how we had to get up well before dawn because we needed to reach the monkeys before they woke up and started moving about. He warned us that if we lost them, it might take ages to find them again.

So it was early to bed, alarm clocks and a hastily grabbed breakfast before we headed off in the dark. We stumbled up beside a stream, boulder-hopped across it repeatedly, till we turned off to climb one of the hills. And that was when our stroll turned into hard work because the mountains of Szechwan are dauntingly steep. Before I came, I'd seen dozens of those Chinese pictures with hills, pine trees and cranes, and I decided that the whole thing had to be symbolic rather than representational because cranes don't sit in pine trees, and hills don't come that steep. I was right about cranes, they never sit in trees, but the hills we were climbing were at least as steep as the ones in the pictures. There was sleet falling, it was very cold and incredibly hard going.

That evening as we struggled back into camp, we had no idea that our arduous day was to be just the first of many. The following days had two things in common. They left us totally exhausted, and we saw no monkeys. It might have been good training for joining the Parachute Regiment, but it didn't seem to have much to do with filming animals. But every day we found signs of the monkeys, and Lo Pen told us he thought he knew where they were headed, so the next day we would start again.

It took about a week for doubt to appear and whisper in my ear that Lo Pen was making it up as he went along. We kept going but with less and less enthusiasm as we set off; with more and more resignation when we got back. Then one morning Lo Pen seemed to set off with more of a spring in his step. We went in a slightly different direction, and the signs of monkeys were obviously more recent. At about mid-day a very excited Lo Pen stopped us and pointed to the far hillside. In the far distance we could see snow capped peaks and on the ridge closest to us, the dark green pine trees had great golden balls in them. The whole ridge looked ready for Christmas, but we all realised that they were monkeys, and half way up the Himalayas at that.

We waited till the monkeys settled down for their after-lunch siesta (I was right, deep down, monkeys are warm climate animals) and then we set off towards them. As quietly as possible we went down one hill and up the next. By now we were used to slipping and sliding down muddy slopes, and crawling our way up them, but because we were trying to go fast and silently, we seemed to take an age, and I was sure we were making more noise than a school outing. When eventually we reached them, the nearest animal gazed at us bleary-eyed when we woke it up.

Golden monkeys are gorgeous creatures, and Chris had totally undersold them. As to the picture Ken had shown me, it was a gross insult. The face that was turned to me was a vivid blue with a little up-turned nose, and the animal's fur was way beyond yellow: it was glorious spun gold that shimmered in the sunlight. Their fur is so golden, so shiny and so long that it looks unnatural, more like a synthetic fur coat or a pantomime costume than the real thing. All around us were these unreal creatures sitting in the pine trees. The occasional youngster was awake and annoying its mother, but the rest were sleeping in the sunshine. One by one they woke up, and the scene became gently animated. Even the adults started climbing around in the trees, and then they began jumping from tree to tree. They are big monkeys so when one landed in a tree, the whole thing shook, waking any animal still trying to sleep there. They started feeding on tree bark and shoots, dropping the remains and leaving the sort of signs that had become so familiar. I was filming away and getting some pretty good results, but I wanted more. They were all around us, and there must have been sixty or seventy all together making a wonderful cacophony of strange noises.

They all seemed quite happy and I thought they had accepted our presence when suddenly a huge commotion broke out. One or two big males had spotted us, and obviously decided that we were dangerous. In a second we were surrounded by hysterical animals screaming at us. They leapt from tree to tree: huge death-defying jumps that tore off whole branches as they landed. Frenzied animals dashed around the place making a hideous racket and tearing bits off the trees. Sticks rained down as the big males bombarded us. It was pandemonium. They seemed to be having a competition to see who could intimidate us the most, and they all made a pretty good job of it.

Meanwhile, the females and youngsters slunk away from the battle zone, slipping down the hill unnoticed from tree to tree, leaving the much larger males to bring up the rear. Soon they broke off the engagement, and charged off leaving us surrounded by a scene of devastation.

We had no chance of following them: they were travelling far faster than we could hope to do, so we just watched them go down the hill, and up the other side of the valley. They finally took up a position on the next ridge, and we could see them in the setting sun, glinting golden balls on the dark green trees with snow covered peaks behind them. And that was the last we saw of them.

That evening in camp the mood was ecstatic. Chris and I sorted out the film we had shot and congratulated ourselves that we had at last managed to film the monkeys. Everybody else prepared a banquet, so that evening, large quantities of food and even larger quantities of drink were consumed.

The drink loosened tongues, and one subject we learned more about was Lo Pen. My worst fears were confirmed when we heard about his upbringing and about a previous camera crew's efforts to film the monkeys. Evidently, Lo Pen's parents were killed during the war by the Japanese army. The Japanese invasion of China penetrated as far as the foothills of the Himalayas including the area we were in. So Lo Pen was brought up by his aunts, with little love for the Japanese.

Two years before we arrived, a Japanese film crew had come to the reserve to film golden monkeys, and Lo Pen had been asked to act as their guide. And that was exactly what he did: he acted as their guide. He took them all over those mountains every day for four weeks. They went up vertiginous slopes, down mudslides and over rivers and they never saw a monkey: they never had a chance. Lo Pen savoured his revenge.

Obviously we hadn't fared too badly by comparison, but

with a little more drink inside him, a rather sheepish Lo Pen confessed that for the first few days he hadn't actually been taking us to the monkeys. He had just been testing us to see if we deserved to see them. Evidently we passed the test so eventually he did take us in the right direction. Even then it had taken several days for him to find them, so not all of our efforts had been in vain.

Initially I was indignant at this revelation, but as I absorbed the meaning of what had happened I found myself respecting Lo Pen more than ever, and I realised that none of our efforts had been in vain. I decided that I like the idea that certain animals are so wonderful that you have to prove yourself worthy before you can be allowed to see them.

CHAPTER SEVENTEEN

Hovering on the Edge
of Insanity

I REMEMBER WATCHING TELEVISION YEARS AGO and seeing a comedian who had dressed himself up as a grotesquely bearded contestant for the crown of Miss World. For the *pièce de résistance*, this unlikely beauty queen was interviewed and asked about her ambitions. A breathless simpering answer came back: 'I want to travel, to help little children and animals and save the world.'

I found I couldn't laugh quite as much as I might have done, because my childhood ambitions weren't that far removed from those platitudes. I wasn't so sure about the little children bit, but I certainly wanted to travel, work with animals and save the world. I saw making wildlife pro-grammes as being my contribution to saving the world from the ecological disasters that hang over us, and I pursued that career avidly.

When eventually I became established as a cameraman, and started to travel widely, my dreams came back to haunt me. The travel bit of my dream was meant to involve driving free and unencumbered around the plains of East Africa, but like most dreams, mine missed out one or two of the steps needed to achieve it. For a start, you have to get to East Africa, and whoever it was said that travel broadens the mind never got stuck at Heathrow airport.

'Unencumbered' was also a laughable idea because it is totally incompatible with filming. I usually set off from home with about twenty cases of equipment, and, to the huge relief of my insurers, I usually manage to get back with about the same number. But in the intervening time those cases become a monstrous ball and chain, a millstone around my neck and a constant source of anxiety. The paperwork alone is enough to cause ulcers, and excess baggage charges make a total mockery of any efforts on a mere human scale to economise.

The worry with all those cases is that they need to be protected from things. To be more accurate they need to be protected from just about everything. Violence can obviously ruin a camera or a lens, so I had to be physically restrained as I watched my kit being unloaded from a plane at Nairobi. One man inside the plane was dropping cases to the tarmac, while his friend threw them onto a trailer. The possibility of opportunistic theft nags like a bad tooth, and like a toothache, there is precious little you can do about it, though 'constant vigilance' becomes a motto. Water is a disaster waiting to swallow cameras, and salt water is an added refinement to that horror. The worry of forgetting a case, or just leaving one behind somewhere turns me obsessive, so I end up counting cases in my sleep. High temperatures destroy film, as can X-rays, so I dread having to run the gauntlet of airport security. I end up like a neurotic mother hen clucking around her brood and exploding in paroxysms of panic every time a new threat comes near.

Eventually I reach my filming destination, but the travelling doesn't stop there. It is no good simply filming in the one spot, so moving around with the equipment opens up whole new areas of possible disaster. Travel in that context ranges from endless dusty trips in four-wheel drive vehicles to occasional bullock carts, from dug-out canoes to helicopters. And if that doesn't broaden your mind, nothing will, though the chief lesson I have learned from my travels is that there is no such thing as a sane helicopter pilot.

This, the First Law of Helicopters, was explained to me many years ago by the first pilot I flew with. His explanation of the First Law is that pilots were all trained in the military, and did most of their early flying in Vietnam. That first pilot, whose name was Mike, met all the requirements of the First Law, but he also explained to me the Second Law, which says that Helicopters Are Incredibly Safe. His argument about safety came out as we plummeted straight down towards the lakes and rocks that make up so much of Canada. He had maximum lift on the rotor, and the engine was howling in agony, but we were still going down. I felt as though I was in the lift of some monster tower block, and a homicidal maniac had taken over the controls.

'The down-draught has to stop before it hits the rocks,' he shouted above the engine's roar, 'so it can't push us underground.'

That sounded fine, but my senses were telling me a different story. The world was coming straight for us. My seat belt was the only thing keeping my skull away from the roof and I was convinced that we were heading for oblivion. But as Mike spoke, our descent slowed and several seconds before we reached the basement funeral parlour, we levelled out and flew away happily.

'It's all these clouds,' Mike explained pointing upwards. 'The column of air right below a cloud goes up, so we go up with it. But then between the clouds, the air's going down, and we go down a bit. Don't worry though, these things are as safe as houses.' He patted the instrument panel in front of us in an affectionate sort of way, and I realised for the first time that at heart Mike was just a cowboy. The difference was that he had a flying horse.

I decided that I could live with the idea of a latter-day flying cowboy, and only became seriously concerned about Mike's sanity when he spotted a moose below us. The first I knew about it was when I was nearly stunned by the whoop that came over my headphones. I recovered from that to realise that we were diving towards a bog that contained the unsuspecting animal. 'I'll show you how we tag 'em.'

With that Mike proceeded to land with one float of our tiny cantilevered goldfish bowl either side of the terrified moose as it tried to thrash its way out of the swamp. 'Now, climb out onto the float, and you can stroke its head.'

I looked at him.

'Go on, do it.' There was no arguing with him, so that was how I came to stroke a live, very wild, moose.

Flying with Mike was part of a research job I had straight after leaving university, and it was a lot of fun. However, since I became a cameraman my early love affair with helicopters has developed and matured. Our relationship has flourished because helicopters often get involved in film shoots.

For one thing, a helicopter is often the only way of getting to places that are seriously off the beaten track. That is a very good description of Franz Joseph Land up in the Arctic, and while I was there with the Austrian expedition we relied quite heavily on helicopters. They came on the scene once we had reached the islands because they took us ashore and gave us occasional logistical support bringing supplies from the Russian mainland. It was a very long flight, so the huge Russian MI8 helicopters equipped with extra fuel tanks were the only machines that could make it.

On the outside, these helicopters looked a bit battered with peeling paint, black exhaust smudges, dents all over the body panels and rear doors vaguely held together with a bent wire coat-hanger. There were odd bits of metal, rolling around or stuck to the floor in a thick deposit of seeping engine oil, spilt coffee and cigarette ends. The cigarette stubs had probably only joined the sediment on the floor when the empty vodka bottle that served as an ashtray had fallen off the navigation table and smashed. As reassurance we were told that these were well-proven planes that had survived long and distinguished service in the Afghan war.

Unfortunately, the bodywork of these helicopters was not the only part of them that had suffered during their long service. 'I am not sure how much we can lift,' explained the pilot as he warmed up the engine in preparation to take us to one of the neighbouring islands. 'The engine does not produce full power. I think it needs servicing. If we can take off, we will be OK.' I rolled around my mind the happy thought of how the passengers would react to this announcement if it came from the captain of a jumbo jet leaving Heathrow, but we did take off, and it was OK.

The finest hour for the MI8 came as it arrived one time and put down on the landing spot we had marked out at the edge of camp. Over the weeks the camp had expanded and developed, so that we now had additional facilities including an extra toilet tent. For obvious reasons we had sited this new luxury at the edge of camp, but nobody noticed that the camp had encroached on the barren area we had marked out as a helicopter-landing site.

On that day, Florian, the sound recordist, innocently entered the new toilet tent. It was pure bad luck that he chose to relieve himself at just the moment when the rest of us heard the sound of a helicopter arriving from the mainland bringing us fresh food. The arrival of fresh supplies was a big event so everybody, except Florian, came out to watch the helicopter. It slowly materialised out of the cloud heading for the landing site and toilet tent in a mighty rushing wind.

That wind proved too much for the recently erected tent as the helicopter closed in on it. First it began to flap, then one by one the guy ropes came unpegged till the whole tent took to the air revealing Florian seated in all his glory. The sudden blast of wind struck our sound-recordist in the face and knocked him off his perch so he followed the tent. Relieved of Florian's weight, the bucket followed him and the tent so all three went barrelling down wind away from the helicopter.

Hidden behind the bucket had been a tidy pile of toilet rolls, and now the blast of wind hit them. They joined the exodus, fluttering after the tent, Florian and the bucket. Within seconds, the camp was festooned with paper. Every tent was decorated. The radio mast blossomed with exotic flowers and the clotheslines collected streamers. As they climbed out of their helicopter, the crew gazed in amazement at the decorations and forty or so people rolling around in fits of laughter.

The chief thing I use helicopters for is aerial filming, capturing those shots that take the viewer floating as in a dream to look down on the place where our story will unfold. Producers love putting these bird's-eye views into their programmes, and they're quite right, because just a few shots like that can give a real feeling for a place. As a result I've hovered like a disembodied spirit over many parts of the world, and I almost always manage to enhance the experience by being violently sick. I try to explain to my disgusted companions that my problem comes from having to look at the world through the viewfinder.

'Just flying in a chopper's fine,' I point out, 'but when I'm filming, I see the world down the viewfinder and it flows smoothly past my eyes. At the same time, my body is tossed about by the turbulence. So I'm sick.'

My record, I think, is about four minutes between take-off and First Vomit. That record-breaking flight was on the lovely Caribbean Island of Dominica. Our pilot there was a Frenchman from the neighbouring island of Martinique and his name was Pierre. Within minutes, he proved that he was, as predicted, mad, and that evening, as I refilled my stomach, he told us about his experience as an instructor for the French Air Force, so my worst fears were confirmed.

Flying over Dominica with Pierre was special for reasons beyond merely setting the four-minute record. In a small helicopter you communicate by talking through the intercom system but even we Englishmen find ourselves using positively Gallic hand gestures for added emphasis. That works fine for everybody except me, the cameraman, because when I am filming, hand gestures are out, and the normal headset with big headphones and a microphone get in the way all the time. But Pierre came to my rescue.

'For you James, a special headset. Only one earpiece, but I think it is enough. And here, a throat microphone, so it's not in the way.'

It looked ideal, so I tried on the single headphone and fixed the microphone round my neck so that it sat on my Adam's apple. Three minutes and forty-five seconds into our first flight I knew I had a problem, so I passed the camera to Sean, my assistant, and pulled out the first of my store of plastic bags. With a normal headset I've learned to get the microphone out of the way as I reach for a plastic bag. But the throat microphone was inconspicuously attached to me, and I didn't think about it for a moment. Until I was actually sick, and that was when the throat microphone came into its own. In hindsight, I realise that I should have turned the volume down on my microphone before I filled my plastic bag. As it was, everybody in the plane was regaled in full stereo with all my heavings and retchings. Pierre was so startled and disgusted that we came as close to crashing as I have ever been.

Pierre's efforts to accommodate me had gone far beyond the special headset. Even as I tried on the headset, I cast a dubious eye at the window because trying to film through the window of a helicopter is deeply frustrating. It restricts you to filming at one angle: always the wrong angle.

'Oh don't worry. We take the door off,' said Pierre dismissing such a trivial problem.

So we unscrewed the door. However, that left me feeling a trifle exposed as I sat in the seat next to the open door. But I had underestimated Pierre.

'Now we take the seat out,' he said. 'That way you can move around.' I tried a smile but it came out a bit wan. 'Oh. And we strap you in with the harness. I don't get paid if I lose the cameraman.'

The last thing we did was to suspend my camera with a set of bunjees from the top of the doorframe. This took the weight and smoothed out most of the helicopter's vibrations. I also attached a safety line to the camera.

'I don't get paid if I lose the camera,' I told Pierre.

So I sat on the floor of the helicopter with my legs dangling out of the hole where the door should have been while Dominica flashed past between my feet. Once I had learned to turn the volume down each time I was sick, we carried on and shot aerials all over the island, so we ended up seeing virtually the whole place from the air. Early on we noted a beautiful river that had cut a canyon through the rock for about three miles, so as a grand finale we decided to film it, flying up the canyon.

For going up the canyon I wanted to sit right out on the landing skid with my legs dangling, so we extended the harness till it held me in roughly the right place. Then I asked Pierre to fly sideways when we flew between the cliffs. The idea was that I could film straight forwards to give the viewer the full drama of the canyon. I carefully avoided using the phrase '... the full impact of the canyon' because, though Pierre's English was excellent, I wanted no misunderstandings about this.

So I found myself strapped onto the side of a helicopter, hurtling sideways up a narrow winding rocky crack in the ground. We twisted and turned between those crags, flying well below the top of the canyon, so there was virtually no sky to be seen, just lots of rock. Down the viewfinder I could see absolutely nothing but stone, and it was all rushing towards me. Huge cliffs whipped past me, and rocky pinnacles flashed between my feet in a dizzying sequence that seemed to go on for ever.

That would have been excitement enough, but what I hadn't allowed for was Pierre's background. It turns out that though he hadn't actually flown in Vietnam, he was an aficionado of films about that war. Especially *Apocalypse Now*. So just to complete the thrill of my white-knuckle ride, Pierre decided to add the soundtrack of his favourite film. The *Ride of the Valkyries* came blasting down my earphone at full volume, and in some frightening way the twists and turns of the helicopter seemed to follow the rhythm of the music. With rising panic I realised that we were flying in six eight time, and the music rather than the cliffs were dictating when we made each turn. I had no time to think how frightening that was because the rest of the crew decided that for added reality, they would provide the machine gun noises, the screams and the howls that should have been on the soundtrack. I was so terrified I even forgot to be sick.

When eventually we landed, I unstrapped myself and staggered out onto the airfield. That flight had convinced me that there is no way of telling whether helicopters are safe or not, but they would be a whole lot safer if it weren't for the undeniable fact that helicopter pilots are totally mad.

CHAPTER EIGHTEEN

Castaway

THE YEAR 1704 WAS A BAD ONE for Alexander Selkirk. It started deceptively well when he won the post of sailing master on a ship called *Cinque Ports* under Captain Thomas Stradling and they joined a 'Privateering' Expedition in the Pacific. But the two soon quarrelled. In high dudgeon, Selkirk demanded to be put ashore when they next made land and, tragically for him, his wish was granted. Their first landfall turned out to be a small island about two hundred miles off the coast of Chile, and the poor man spent the next five years entirely alone on the island.

After his rescue and eventual return to England, Selkirk had a brief moment of fame, before declining into penury, dereliction and obscurity, but his story inspired a book.

Mysteriously, the author chose to move the action from the Pacific to the Caribbean. He also used his artistic licence to add marauding savages and a companion named Man Friday. The author was of course Daniel Defoe, and the book was his major novel, *Robinson Crusoe*. The island that Selkirk was stuck on, Juan Fernandez, is now popularly known as Robinson Crusoe Island in honour of the book that his exploits inspired.

To reach the island now is a little easier than it was three hundred years ago, but it is still a bit off the tourist trail. There's a small and unreliable boat that makes the journey occasionally, taking supplies to the islanders. The alternative is a small and unreliable plane that takes visitors to the island. We chose the plane.

The plane we were to travel in was a twin engine aircraft that had just six seats. It was the only plane owned by an airline whose sole route was from Santiago to Robinson Crusoe Island. A charming lady at the desk sold us our tickets, and then collected them straight back from us. It was a lovely little formality because we had been through roughly the same performance the day before. That was because we had tried to fly to the island the day before. We had also tried to fly the day before that, and the day before that as well. In fact we had been trying to fly there for the better part of a week, but the weather kept closing in and we gathered that the airport on the island didn't have instrument landing capability.

The whole ceremony of the tickets was also rather quaint because there weren't that many passengers. In fact William, myself and the camera gear took up all five passenger seats, leaving just enough room for the pilot, Ramon, who turned out to be the ticket-lady's husband.

Eventually Ramon got a weather report from the island that included words like 'sunny spells' and 'bright periods', or their Spanish equivalents, so he decided that at last we could take off. As we cleared the coast we met huge billowing clouds, and Ramon had to thread his way round them one after another. Below us the Pacific was cold, grey and rough. An hour into the flight, Ramon started fumbling for something under his seat, and I feared we were going to have to turn back yet again. But after a couple of minutes scrabbling around on the floor, Ramon solemnly turned to William and me, and handed us a little package each. This was cabin service as offered by Air Robinson Crusoe, and we both gleefully opened our in-flight snacks, doubtless made by our cheerful ticket lady.

After a couple of hours flying we found the island, and my sympathy for Selkirk grew. It wasn't just a bit isolated; it was bleak, dark and forbidding, with huge cliffs rising straight out of the ocean. Then I spotted the landing strip. It was perched on top of one of the huge cliffs, and although it looked horribly short, there was no way it could have been any longer. It stretched all the way across the island's only bit of flat ground from the precipice on one side of the island to the precipice on the other, a few hundred metres away. And we had been told it lacked instrument landing capability. I needed convincing that it had any landing capability at all.

Ramon circled and went in for his approach, but not

before he had given his passengers a good clear view of how small the landing strip was, and how easy it would be to over-shoot it. At least, he said he was going in for his approach, but I knew better. Ramon had decided to end it all and fly straight into the cliff. Being proprietor of the smallest semi-commercial airline in Chile had obviously taken its toll – the cancellations, the weather, the price of fuel had become more than he could bear. He said not another word but aimed the plane at a spot some twenty metres below the top of the cliff, and went for it. My only consolation was that it would look like an accident, so Ramon's charming widow would be able to collect the insurance. So would mine.

I could see nothing but the cliff as it loomed up ahead of us. While we rushed headlong to our doom, I tried to ignore our predicament and marvel instead at the different rock types and their colours. As we got closer, I could make out plants clinging to the cliffs. I knew they were strange, unique plants, and we had come all this way to film them, but my attention was wandering. The cliff was getting closer. By the time I could count the petals on the flowers, I couldn't ignore my impending death much longer.

With all the decisiveness of a rabbit caught in head-lights, I pointed wordlessly at the cliff in case Ramon hadn't noticed it. Then, just as my life lined itself up ready to flash before me, the plane gently rose till we cleared the top of the cliff and miraculously we were looking along the tiny landing strip. We touched down – it wasn't gentle but it wasn't fatal either. Then we were racing towards the precipice and the drop to the sea below. But we slowed down and Ramon turned to give us a broad grin. Later, William and I were able to nod sagely and talk about up-draughts and cliffs, but for a while things had not looked promising.

'Welcome to Robinson Crusoe Island,' said Ramon but all I could manage was an incoherent nod by way of reply.

The arrivals hall at Robinson Crusoe Island Airport consisted of a little wooden tool shed with a broken window. Beside it was the waiting area – a seat that, at some time in the dim and distant past, must have been jettisoned by a car in its death throws.

I looked around me. It was cold, barren and windy, and it started to rain.

'What on earth are we doing here?' I asked William.

'It's the plants, isn't it. Remember? Strange, rare endemic plants. That's what we're here for. Look, here's a plant. We'll film it – well, we may have to wait for the sun to come out. But there are lots of plants here. That's good.' William was one of the most reliably up-beat people I have worked with, and just at that moment I must have been one of his most taxing audiences.

While William and I unloaded the equipment, Ramon set about siphoning fuel out of the plane into a can that he had collected from the shed. He climbed up a small hill to a very dilapidated four-wheel drive vehicle of indeterminate vintage and poured the fuel into it. I soon realised why the car had been left on the hill rather than by the arrivals hall, because Ramon released the break and pushed the car down the hill towards the plane. He jumped in and a roar from the unsilenced engine announced that the aviation fuel had reached the cylinders.

'Oh, look. Our courtesy coach. Good.' William, of course. I was still in no mood for idle banter.

With the equipment and ourselves in the car, Ramon drove us down a precipitous track cut into the cliff. At the foot of the cliff was the most perfect little harbour containing one small boat, and twenty fur seals playing about in the water. They were so beautiful and alive that they revived my optimism a notch or two.

'Look,' I managed to say, 'let's film fur seals. They are rare and much more fun than plants.'

'No, James,' replied William in his best schoolmaster voice. 'Remember Tony is filming them. We are here to film the plants, and they are very exciting.'

'Yes, William,' was all I could manage.

The harbour was an almost exact circle of vertical cliffs with a single narrow outlet to the ocean, and seeing it I started to get a bit more positive about things. As well as filming the plants, we also had to cover the island's origin, so we needed images that showed how it came to be there at all.

About five million years ago a volcano blasted itself up from the ocean floor, and didn't stop till it was over three thousand metres clear of the water. Looking at that harbour it struck me that it was the clearest evidence imaginable of that marine volcano and the origin of this isolated island. Our harbour must have been one of the small side vents of the volcano. In fact it was so perfect it looked like a diagram from a textbook, so I made a mental note to come back and film it.

In the meantime I turned my attention to our boat. It was about six metres long and open except for a small fore deck. The rest of the boat was full of a huge pile of old tarpaulins.

'I asked them to bring tarpaulins,' said William, 'they should help keep the cameras dry.'

'Good thinking,' I replied as I started to heave camera cases towards the boat.

We all set about wrapping cases in canvas as carefully as we could, and putting them in the boat. Only a few of my cases are totally waterproof, so we had to make sure they were all out of the bilges as well as covering them from the top.

With hindsight I know I should have seen the danger signals. Bilges awash, tarpaulins to cover the equipment and the boat owner wearing oilskins that glistened from head to toe; these things should have warned me. But the harbour looked placid, and what I could glimpse of the open sea looked reasonable, so I ignored the warning signs. I'm a hopeless sailor, but I climbed aboard with hardly a worry. I was just pleased to be out of the cramped kamikaze plane and the smelly car.

As we left the harbour the cliffs loomed over us like the scenery of an early Hammer Horror film. Dracula's castle would have looked good perched on top of them. From the air they had looked big, but from sea level they were enormous, and for Selkirk they must have been real prison walls. From the base of those awesome cliffs, it was easy to believe the account of how a volcano thrust up out of the sea. Except of course that sea level was nowhere near the bottom of the cliffs: they went on down for thousands more metres to the bottom of the sea and we were looking at less than half of the volcano.

Having a volcanic origin does something for an island. At birth it rises smoking and sterile out of the waves with not a living thing on it. As it cools it is colonised, but anything that lives there must have ancestors that crossed the sea to reach it. That journey is always hazardous, as I felt we had just proved, so most volcanic islands are home to an odd assortment of plants and animals, and Robinson Crusoe Island is no exception. Sea birds are usually the first animals to arrive, and the first we saw were albatrosses wheeling effortlessly above the waves.

As we left the harbour, I tried to spot some of the island's strangest inhabitants, its rare endemic flowers. From the boat I could gaze up at the cliffs, and search for plants through binoculars – or I could till we rounded the headland. Then the full force of the misnamed Pacific hit us. The tarpaulins came into their own, and I burrowed under them to find my personal case and extract my waterproofs from it. Once I was properly dressed I could get back to plant spotting. That was the idea, but within minutes I was leaning over the side passing on my in-flight snack to the fishes.

The only good thing about being seasick is that you recover from it quite quickly. So, soon after we landed, I started to take notice and realised that the village of Robinson Crusoe is sweet, with its little houses clustered round the harbour. Most of the streets are unpaved and because it rains so much, they are largely mud. And there along the main street was what I had been looking for: daisy trees. They stood three or four metres tall, with big leaves and huge yellow flowers. Obviously, some type of daisy had been one of the first arrivals on the island, and they had evolved in less than five million years into these full size trees. It wasn't only daisies that flourished and evolved on the island; there are dozens of endemic plants, and not just species of plants, there are entire groups that occur nowhere else. There is even one whose only known relative was found in Namibia as a fossil from eighty million years ago. The island is to a botanist what the Galapagos Islands are to a zoologist.

It was some time before I realised why there were daisy trees lining the high street. It turns out that the Chilean conservation organisation that looks after the island encourages the villagers to have these native plants in their gardens, because they're so badly threatened in the rest of the island. Ironically the threat to the plants comes from the very thing that allowed Selkirk, the island's first human inhabitant, to survive for five years. In the seventeenth century the Royal Navy realised that its men might at some time become marooned on any one of the little islands dotted all over the Pacific, so they had a policy of installing a precautionary food supply for these future castaways. They introduced goats to dozens of islands, and lucky for Selkirk that they did because goat became his staple food. However, it is one thing to have goats on the island; it is quite another to have goat to eat. The only way Selkirk could kill a goat was to chase it across the cliffs till it fell to its death, and goats are no mean rock-climbers.

Today the descendants of those naval goats are still on the island, and like goats everywhere they eat anything that grows. More recently the goats had reinforcements in the shape of rabbits that were also introduced to the island, and between them these two pests have reduced the unique flora of the island close to extinction. Helping them in their destructive ambition is another unlikely threat to the native plants – brambles. These were introduced accidentally, probably in a jar of bramble jelly, and they have turned about a fifth of the island into an impenetrable jungle.

William and I were on the island chiefly to film its unique flora, and a few of the animals that have evolved in parallel with the plants. Many of the plants are only just hanging on, literally in some cases because their last refuge is on the cliffs, where even the goats can't reach them. Filming them was a painfully slow job involving ropes and climbing gear as well as the usual delays waiting for the sun to come out, and the wind to drop. The most convenient place for this was at a point on the island's central ridge called 'Selkirk's Lookout'. The story goes that he collected a great stack of dry wood there, ready for a fire if ever he spotted a passing ship out to sea. It is also said that he climbed to the lookout daily, and if that is true, it confirms both his desperation and his fitness.

The first time we went up there, we struggled with cameras, tripods and lenses on our backs, so we arrived dripping with sweat and barely able to appreciate the view. The second time we were wiser, and hired a mule to carry all the gear. The mule's owner happily went on strapping more and more equipment to the animal's back, saying confidently that his beast could carry anything. It was a matter of pride with him, and with slight reservations, we went along with his bravado.

As the track wound up the hill, it became narrower and steeper, but with the mule ahead of me, I could enjoy the freedom of not having a pack on my back. Each corner we turned revealed more cliffs and bays so the view just kept getting better. Suddenly from up ahead came shouts and anguished noises from the mule. I rounded a corner to be confronted by the sight of the mule lying on its back on top of all my kit and kicking its feet in the air like a stranded tortoise. The path had become so steep that all the baggage had made the poor animal top heavy and it had toppled over backwards. We cut the ropes tying everything onto the saddle and released the poor animal. From there to the top we shared the burden with a rather sulky mule and a chastened mule owner.

From the ridge the view was breathtaking and confirmed that Selkirk had chosen his lookout well. The island stretched away from us with cliffs of fragmented rock falling into the ocean. Those cliffs are now only about a third of the height they reached when the island was born, but, in places, they still plunge almost a thousand metres straight down. This scenery provided a wonderfully dramatic background for the plants that we were filming, the strange relatives of the daisies, and the tree ferns that managed to reach this island from New Zealand. The cliffs emphasised the isolation of the place perfectly.

It was while I was up at Selkirk's Lookout filming the plants that I received news from home. Crispin, the producer on the programme we were filming had planned to have a day catching up with his paper work in the village, but he suddenly appeared flushed and out of breath as he came up the hill to join us. As soon as I saw him my heart sank because I knew why he was there. My father had been ill for some time, but the reports had spoken of his condition being stable, and even pointed to his recovery. Now I learned that he had suffered a sudden relapse, and had died the night before. It would be hard to imagine a bleaker place to hear such news.

The next morning I took the boat from the village to the landing strip, the little plane to the mainland, and then, with barely a pause, I flew from Santiago to New York. I had a six-hour wait in New York before I could board my onward flight to London, so, having time to kill, I took the bus into Manhattan.

Anybody wanting to experience serious disorientation would be well advised to follow my example on that journey. Start by spending a month or so on Robinson Crusoe Island wandering around the windblown cliffs and watching the endless empty ocean and the albatrosses. Then go directly to the Isle of Manhattan. I was there physically, but all I could do was gaze around me at those huge buildings with my mind still full of even bigger cliffs and a roaring turbulent sea. The congested streets made me think of the daisy trees and I suddenly developed enormous sympathy for Selkirk when he returned to London. Travel might broaden the mind, but sometimes it takes a bit of time for your mind to catch up with your body.

CHAPTER NINETEEN

Life, Death and Taxes

By THE AGE OF NEARLY FIFTY I thought I had a
fairly clear idea of what happens at a funeral.
For a start, there is a body in a coffin. Then there are brave
but softly sobbing relatives, condolences from friends, and
solemn music till finally the coffin is lowered into a grave
or it sombrely slips behind respectful curtains to be cre-
mated later. It all seemed unquestionable, right and natural.
Until I went to Madagascar. If death is seen in the West as a
tragic cause of grief, then in Madagascar it is seen as a huge
and magnificent career move, because in Madagascar dead
ancestors rule.

I discovered this when I was in Madagascar to make two
programmes about the island. These programmes were
intended to take the strange and unique natural history as a

starting point, and to look at the people of the island in relation to it. It is always difficult to combine people and wildlife in programmes, and over the years a range of different styles have been tried. At one extreme there are images of 'primitive' natives living in Rouseau-like harmony with nature. In complete contrast there are campaigning programmes that show the glories and fascination of the natural world, and then blast the comfortable beauty away by showing the horrors of what Man is doing to his environment. We were trying for something a little more balanced than either of these, showing the way that the wildlife of Madagascar and the humans living on the island are inextricably reliant on each other, and the future of the one depends on the future of the other.

Before I went there, I read everything I could find about the wildlife of Madagascar, but I found very little on the people there, so I failed to appreciate how rich the human culture is, or how much of it centres on death. Death hangs over the island. But it's not oppressive: it's just that the people of the island are aware of death in a way that we in the West are not.

The island boasts large, active Christian churches and well-filled mosques, but the underlying belief is still ancestor worship. This starts to manifest itself before death, so, as a person ages, he or she becomes increasingly respected. At forty-eight, I still aggressively refused to think of myself as being at all old, but suddenly I was being treated as if I was quite important, which made a pleasant change. However, for real status, age is not enough, one has to be dead. Dead ancestors are thought of as controlling events for the living, so they must be shown huge respect.

Our first brush with death came in the north of the island, where we attended and filmed a Crocodile ceremony. We first heard about this from the village priest, a rather sad Swiss man who had lived in the village for over twenty years, but still had photos of skiing stars on his office walls. Despite his best efforts, there was a belief in the village that the ancestors were present in the form of crocodiles in the nearby lake. He had even given up preaching against this heresy, and I think that the poor man's sorrow stemmed from this compromise as much as from the perennial lack of snow.

The belief in the crocodiles as ancestors meant that the lake where the crocodiles lived, and the area around it were sacred and totally protected. It wasn't an officially declared nature reserve, but once crocodiles are protected in a lake, other protection measures are unnecessary. The whole area was as well guarded as any conservationist could wish, and it was heaving with wildlife. The villagers made regular offerings to these crocodile-ancestors so as to keep on the right side of them. In addition to the regular ceremonies, individuals in the village with a particular problem could organise a sacrifice on an auspicious day, so as to persuade the ancestors to grant specific requests, and one of these was due soon after we arrived.

On the appointed day, the whole village (except the Swiss priest) danced the two or three kilometres to the lake behind a wonderful band and a handful of lead singers. In the middle of the procession was a bullock, blissfully ignorant of the meaning of this fiesta. By comparison, the crocodiles knew full well that singing and dancing foretold a good meal, so they lined up along the bank at the usual spot and waited. They were good size crocodiles, and scanning along the array of mean grinning teeth, I wondered how the villagers could possibly see them as ancestors. They were hardly my idea of grandparents, and I wondered how on earth these people could see them that way. There was no time to resolve the mystery, because the ceremony seemed to be starting.

At the edge of the lake, the shaman delivered a short speech to the crowd. I filmed him while Chris recorded his every word and it all sounded most impressive. That evening we asked Seraphin, our interpreter and fixer, to translate it for us, and it turned out that what we had filmed was no invocation to the ancestors: the shaman had been telling the villagers about the film crew who were making him and their village so famous.

After the speech, the shaman blessed the bullock by pouring a little rum onto its horns while the animal lay immobile on the ground with its legs tied together. Its terrified eye flickered around the scene and the sacrificial knife lay across its throat. Seraphin had told us about this central event of the ceremony in advance and I had managed to position myself right by the bullock's head at the critical moment. I filmed the shaman as he watched the bullock. Evidently he was waiting for the spirits to enter the animal, because only then could the sacrifice take place. Everybody watched in tense expectant silence.

After about a minute of waiting, watching and filming, the bullock twitched, gave a heave and started to struggle on the ground. This was the sign the shaman had been waiting for, so he picked up the knife and expertly slit the animal's throat. The crowd erupted in a chorus of delighted singing, clapping and dancing, and the crocodiles crept a little farther up the bank. Blood spurted everywhere, and for a minute or so everything I filmed seemed to be slightly fuzzy with a reddish tint to it. Eventually I realised what had happened and cleaned the blood off the front of my lens.

The shaman himself sliced the first bit of flesh off the still twitching carcass and threw it towards the crocodiles. While it was still in mid-air two monsters charged out of the water to catch it. They both grabbed it at the same moment and thrashed about in the shallows till one of them got control of the morsel, and swallowed it. That 'morsel' must have been about five kilos of beef, which gave a scale to the crocs we were dealing with: they were big, and they were hungry.

For the next few minutes, the crocodiles enjoyed a feeding frenzy as a barrage of meat rained down on them. A dozen or so monsters fighting for each lump of bleeding beef soon turned the shallows to red foam. Their frenzy was matched by the excitement of the crowd who interrupted their singing and dancing with great shouts of joy every time an ancestor caught a flying joint of meat. I learned later that the eager way the crocodiles fought to take the offerings showed the villagers that the ancestors were well pleased and would continue to help the village in future. This must have come as quite a relief given the alternative suggested by ancestors with teeth and jaws like these.

Philip, who had so enlivened my trip to the Arctic, was the second cameraman with me in Madagascar, so there were two of us trying to film the ceremony, and it definitely needed both of us. We had tried to plan what we would do the night before, but nothing had prepared us for the speed of events once the action started. There were pieces of beef flying everywhere, crocodiles fighting, ad hoc butchers dismembering the bullock, dancers, singers, dogs fighting over the scraps: it was a scene of excited happy chaos. During the height of the drama, Philip went for the lakeside and spent his time dodging flying meat and keeping out of the reach of the crocodiles. Those ancestors made it plain that they would have been quite happy to include him as part of their feast.

I chiefly covered the butchery party where the carcass was fast being dismembered under the gaze of the shaman. They did an expert job, so in no time at all the whole bullock had been reduced to manageable joints of meat. Certain parts of the carcass were offered to the crocodile ancestors, other portions were wrapped up in the skin and loaded onto a cart for the living villagers to eat that evening. By my reckoning, the living got the better end of the deal but that still left the crocodiles about a hundred kilos of beef to fight over.

Both Philip and I tried to cover the crowd, who, like a Greek chorus, provided a continuous excited background to the drama being enacted at the water's edge. Throughout the proceedings, the band played enthusiastic but slightly ragged music, the crowd sang along with the band and the dancers followed the complicated rhythms. The dancing was exuberant with a great deal of stamping and body waving and just a touch of co-ordination as the half dozen or so dancers followed the lead of a particularly attractive young woman. She flirted outrageously with Philip, as almost every woman we met seemed to do, which meant that he got some lovely shots of her.

When the bullock had been totally butchered, the serious part of the ceremony began. The shaman took the bullock's skull into a little fenced off enclosure, and put it on top of a pole. It joined a considerable collection of other skulls on poles; mute testament to the devotion these people had paid to their ancestors over the years. I felt like a leper because I was barred from this holy of holys, but everyone was happy for me to film the ceremony through the gaps in the bamboo screen. Philip's beautiful, young dancing star followed the shaman to this sacred spot, and started getting him to pass on her requests to the increasingly well-fed ancestors.

Coming from a vaguely Church of England background, I suppose I expected this time of prayer to be greeted with hushed respect, but I couldn't have been more wrong. The band played on, the crowd sang louder, and if anything, the remaining dancers became more frenzied. This added excitement just might have been spurred on by the fact that somebody broached a barrel of rum at about this stage. When we had asked the day before if there was any way we could contribute to the festivities, the reply came back that some rum would be appreciated, and the drink appeared as soon as the bullock had been totally dismembered. Forty litres was the suggested amount, and it was rough, powerful stuff so it had quite an impact on the assembled villagers. Forty litres of rum also duly appeared on our expense claim, to the confusion of the accountants.

All this time the crocodiles cruised along the edge of the lake obviously hoping for another course of their feast. Their wish was almost granted when one young man became blind drunk and decided to go and talk to his dead uncle personally. Friends grabbed him just before the crocodiles did, and then took turns to restrain him. After a while they got bored with their task, and tied him to a tree, where he sang himself to sleep in the sun.

Eventually the festivities broke up, and everybody started drifting back to the village. I got Seraphin to ask our star dancer just before she left if she would be attending Mass the following day. I wanted to film her taking communion from the Swiss priest to show the way that people in Madagascar have mixed traditional and introduced beliefs. Her reply had a rounded beauty to it.

'Why would I go to church?' she asked, and then added, 'I'm a Muslim. I went to Friday prayers yesterday.'

Filming the crocodile ceremony made us realise how vitally important are death and the rituals surrounding death in Madagascar. They certainly made up the most vivid set of experiences of our time there but I don't want to give the impression that we went around the island like a coven of ghouls looking for corpses. On the contrary, the wildlife of Madagascar was the basis of our film because it is exceptional, and it desperately needs conservation.

From the biological point of view, Madagascar demands very special consideration and filming the wildlife was very exciting. There are so many plants and animals that only occur there, that the island is virtually a continent. The lemurs are perhaps the best known of these endemic animals, and we filmed many of them. Lemurs are primitive primates that are related to the ancestors of monkeys and apes, but those more advanced groups have totally displaced lemur-like animals in the rest of the world. Their presence in Madagascar points to the fact that the island was separated from mainland Africa rather over a hundred million years ago, before the more advanced primates evolved. It is this long separation from the rest of the world that makes the island and its wildlife unique.

Fortunately, some of the rare endemic species are protected by taboos. So, for instance, the island is the world headquarters for chameleons with about eighty species found only on the island. Chameleons are generally taboo, or 'Fadi' as it is called in Madagascar, so most people refuse to touch them let alone eat them, and they are left in peace. There are also areas, like the Crocodile Lake, that are protected by religious belief. Some of the conservation organisations encourage and support people in their taboos because this can protect particular species or areas. However, driving around the country we soon realised that these conservation efforts were like spitting in a hurricane. The island as a whole is being destroyed by a rising tide of population growth and poverty. Over-population is followed by deforestation, which leads to massive erosion. Most of the rivers run red as the island bleeds into the Indian Ocean. It is a tragic scene, and we were there to record the island's pain. Fortunately, we were also there to record the island's glory, and we filmed some of the most beautiful sights and quite the most fascinating events I have witnessed.

Three or four months after the crocodile ceremony, our quest took us to the far south of Madagascar, to a little village squeezed between the desert and the sea. We were on the trail of death again because we had heard that the village headman had died and we hoped to film his funeral.

We arrived a few days before the funeral itself, so as to settle in and familiarise ourselves with the place. We met the new headman of the village, a position he had inherited from his brother. He was a very likeable, gentle person who exhibited a genuine concern for the people of the village. He exhibited all the gravitas of a village elder and his new responsibility sat well on his shoulders.

My initial reaction to filming events as emotionally charged as a funeral was one of huge diffidence. I would have hated to have a film crew turn up for my father's funeral, so why should these people accept us?

'They would love you to come,' said Seraphin in response to my anxieties.

'But we must ask permission to film the funeral,' I said. 'They might not want us, so they could make life very difficult. And we could ruin the ceremony, and I really don't want to offend them.'

'No. No,' he replied. 'They will be very happy for us to be there. The more people the better.'

'Maybe, but we must ask.'

So against his better judgement, Seraphin went and asked the dead man's relatives if they minded us filming the funeral. Fortunately he came back smiling, so I knew we were in the clear.

'They are very happy for us to be there,' said Seraphin. 'The big thing with a funeral in my country is that it is a time for everybody to show respect. Having a film crew there will show great respect. That only happens to Hollywood stars and famous statesmen, so we are going to turn the funeral into a very big event. They are very happy.'

'OK. So we just have to turn the dead man into a world star.'

'Yes, but James, please remember something. We don't say that a person is dead. We say that he has turned his back.'

Seraphin was probably the best guide, mentor, interpreter and fixer I've ever worked with, and he did a valiant job of mediating between us and the people we were trying to work with and film. That was just as well because we started out with very little understanding of what lay behind the events we were filming.

While talking to the headman, Seraphin managed to establish that we had the right date, but learned nothing more about the forthcoming ceremony. We had arrived three days before the date of the funeral because we thought we might be able to film the preparations, but nobody seemed to be making any preparations. The exception was a small group of craftsmen sitting under a tree quietly carving totem poles. It was beautiful intricate work they were doing, and we gathered round to watch them and film what they were doing.

We learned that these were craftsmen who moved from village to village always arriving a few days before a big funeral to carve totem poles for the grave. This meant they were well-travelled men, and, unlike the village people, they had often seen television so they had a good idea what we were doing. They were as curious about us as we were about them but eventually Seraphin managed to agree a compromise. We spent half an hour showing them our cameras and tape recorders and so on. They then agreed to spend half an hour showing us how they did their carving so that we could film them.

They were very skilled, and a joy to watch. The totem poles they were creating are a major feature of the district, and each one tells of a man's life. We watched them carve one pole topped with a magnificent bull: below it the master craftsman added a house and several people. These symbols all had a specific meaning, so we got Seraphin to decode them for us. The carved bull was by far the commonest, and it celebrated the wealth of the dead man. The house told of the headman's high status in the village, and the rows of people showed his children: five sons and six daughters. Another of the poles our carvers had created for the funeral showed a motorbike, which told of the dead man's journey to the north end of the island.

The language of the totems is intriguing, because each pole is unique. I became fascinated by them on our journey down to the village, and we stopped to film quite a few of the more eccentric: only now did we learn what half of them meant. We had filmed totems crowned with carved bicycles, rifles, cars and aeroplanes, and most of those were fairly self-explanatory. One showed a man with a crocodile biting off his leg and another showed a man with his arm in a sling. But there was one recurrent motif that I couldn't work out. It looked like a rectangle with the top and bottom lines slightly bowed inwards. A grinning Seraphin explained that it was a bed, and signified that the honoured man had been a renowned lover; not an epitaph I have often seen on English gravestones.

Apart from the carvers, there seemed to be nothing going on in the way of preparation for the big day. Children played in the dust, men talked in the shade of the trees, and women fed chickens or washed clothes: it was a very ordinary sleepy village.

Then on the day before the funeral, it all changed. One after another, groups of people arrived from the neighbouring villages. Each group came and presented itself to the new headman and his assembled brothers, who held court under a tree. An orator from each group intoned a eulogy to the great man, finally telling the family what gift his village had brought to honour the spirit of the man who had turned his back.

Men carrying spears surrounded every orator, and there was a huge amount of general banter between all concerned. Public speaking is highly esteemed in Madagascar, so the assembled company judged the orators pretty shrewdly. The funeral gifts were also judged, but they were generally deemed acceptable because most were gifts of cattle – the most highly prized of possessions in Madagascar – and soon there were beasts tied up under most of the trees in the village. Throughout the island men count their wealth in terms of the number of cattle they own, hence the carved bulls on the totem poles. The gifts were living testament to the importance of the village and its old headman, but I had a shrewd idea that the cattle weren't going to be living testament to anything for very much longer.

Our contribution had a familiar ring to it as far as we were concerned. Since we had no cattle, it was suggested that we should bring some rum, and, once again, the quantity mentioned was forty litres. I started to wonder if, like the forty days in the wilderness, forty litres was a symbolic quantity. Seraphin made a brief speech explaining to the company that we were going to tell people all around the world about their brother who had turned his back. He obviously made a good job of it because wide smiles beamed round at us. When finally he reached the bit about the rum, a huge cheer went up. Our contribution was warmly accepted and put under the protection of the brothers.

That evening I suspect that the immediate family broached the rum: certainly the singing and noise pointed to a happy gathering. Quite early in the evening I asked Seraphin to try and find out what was planned for the next day, and when it was all going to happen. About an hour later, he came back with more than a hint of rum on his breath, and a classic answer to my query.

'I have spoken to the three brothers of the man who has turned his back because they are in charge of the funeral,' he announced. 'One said that the ceremony will start just after dawn, the next that it will start at mid-day, and the third that it will be just before sunset. Nobody would tell me what will happen.' It sounded to me like a fairy story or a child's early reader, but its meaning was clear: we just had to accept that we were not going to be let in on the plans.

We were up before dawn, and there was an air of feverish activity already. By the time the sun rose at least a dozen cattle had had their throats cut. There was blood everywhere and excited children were running about carrying odd bits of carcass. Overnight, every woman in the village seemed to have become an expert butcher. They were carving their way into a beef mountain, and starting fires to get it all cooked. Dogs had a field day, and there was so much food that they even gave up fighting. As the day warmed up, kites came wheeling round the sky swooping on scraps that had been thrown out.

Bearing in mind Seraphin's information about the funeral itself we decided to get ready for the 'just after dawn' starting time. We had no idea of what was going to happen, so my unthinking understanding of funerals came into its own. There is a body in its coffin, I told myself. This had to be key to the proceedings, so I decided to find out where the body was and take it from there. I quizzed Seraphin, and he told us that the body was in the hut where the man used to live, and had been there since he died – about four months ago.

'Four months!' I said.

'In this heat!' added Chris.

'Yes. They had to make all the arrangements, and choose an auspicious date.'

I never did discover how they preserved the body for four months, because at that moment a bullock cart appeared, and it had a handsomely carved coffin on it. I followed the cart till it stopped just outside a house, and Seraphin told me that this was indeed the house where the body was lying. I had located a coffin and now I knew where the body was. A good start, I told myself as I positioned myself near the coffin. I felt secure that nothing much could happen without me filming it.

By now the day was heating up nicely towards 'slow roast', and people started to gather just in front of me, near the house. Some young men arrived with a fine collection of home made musical instruments, and started playing and singing under the tree that had shaded the reception line the day before. The musicians were soon surrounded by the youth of the assembled villages, and they all started chatting and singing along with the impromptu band.

A short distance to my right, the men started to gather.

They totally ignored the youth band just near them, and began their own singing and dancing. Their more traditional singing was dominated by a menacing rhythmic grunting. They shook their spears and stamped in the sand in time with their song, raising clouds of dust. Off to my left a group of women started singing and dancing as well. Theirs was gentler ululating music with slow swaying movements interrupted by occasional bottom-wiggling contests. The total effect was glorious musical anarchy.

To general amusement and approval we set about filming all of this, especially the bottom-wiggling, and our antics only contributed to the general mood of festival. Everybody was having a good time. I clung resolutely to my ideas about the roles of coffins, bodies and solemnity, so I stuck to my position next to the bullock cart. I nurtured an image of the cart carrying the coffin at the head of a solemn procession of quiet mourners that slowly wound its way along the dusty track to the cemetrey.

The 'just after dawn' kick-off time was long gone, and 'about mid-day' had brought nothing but singing, dancing and dust, but sometime during the afternoon a second bullock cart arrived. Into this were loaded the skulls of the cattle that had already been slaughtered in memory of the dead man. On top of these were placed the totem poles that we had watched being carved. We knew that the skulls and the totem poles were destined to be the ornaments on top of the grave, so seeing them all assembled I was sure that the proceedings would be starting fairly soon. We waited out in the blazing sun, but nothing happened. It was only the next day that Seraphin discovered why there was such secrecy about the plans for the funeral.

'If everybody knew what was going to happen,' he said, 'enemies of the village could spoil things. And remember that the enemies could be either living or dead.'

All afternoon people drifted about, and there seemed no particular plan of action, till suddenly at about four o'clock, the gentle festival atmosphere turned to bedlam. A tremendous noise erupted from the house till the whole building swayed. Bits fell off the roof, and it looked as though the wall facing me and the coffin was being torn down.

Seraphin was with me and explained. 'The body has to leave the house in this direction. It's north-east, and the spirit world is in this direction.' The thing that Seraphin hadn't thought to mention was that the door was the other side of the house. He probably took that for granted because houses in Madagascar never have doors facing north-east: it's unlucky as it would give such easy access to the spirits. It was only when I put these facts together that I understood what was happening. The body had to leave the house travelling north-east. There was no door in that direction, so the relatives had to demolish the wall, and that was just what they were doing.

'If the whole house falls down it doesn't matter,' said Seraphin. 'Nobody will live in it now anyway.'

As I watched, the sticks, leaves and mud that made up the house started to fly in all directions till it looked as though a tornado had hit it, and soon the whole wall came down. Through the dust and debris of the house a throng of young men exploded towards me, carrying a man-size bundle above their heads and looking for all the world like the SAS ending a hostage siege. They charged off screaming and shouting, and the crack troops turned into the winning team at the cup final taking the trophy on a lap of honour.

They passed the coffin and me with not a glance in our direction so I set off after them. So much for my predictions about coffins, bodies and solemnity. Chasing them soon became pointless, because by the time I had sorted out the camera, they were coming back again. They completed a circuit of a couple of houses, and raced up to the big tree near where they had started.

As dramatically as it had begun, the excitement stopped. The manic pallbearers put the body down in front of three old women, and stood silently.

'These are the wife and sisters of the man who has turned his back,' Seraphin explained as I filmed this quiet moment.

Together under the shade of the tree, the women and the body created a tableau that briefly resembled my concept of a funeral. Their grief was very apparent, but suddenly a commotion away to our right interrupted my moment of comprehension. Waves of noise broke over us with shouting, whistling and the thunder of cattle hooves. From behind the ruined house a full-scale stampede bore down on us. About a hundred cattle at full gallop crashed through the crowd and the village, urged on by one and all. By some miracle nobody was killed in the stampede.

Watching and trying to film the cattle, we all totally

missed the moment when the arrival of the cattle flipped a switch in the minds of the body bearers. They instantly reverted to mania, picked up the body, abandoned the grieving women, and set off again at a run, whooping and shouting as they went. A trail of mourners straggled after them, but I noticed that the older ones set off walking slowly up the path towards the graveyard. By contrast, the body party was charging round in the bush, running in endless circles, so the tortoise-style older mourners were keeping up with the shouting and chanting hare-like gang with the body. At about this stage the two bullock carts set off plodding slowly and solemnly up the road.

Philip was doing a great job of filming the exuberant procession, so I piled into the Land Cruiser, and drove to the graveyard to film the arrival. The grave site consisted of an area of about four or five metres square that had been cleared of stones. The graves nearby were about this size, and the finished structures consisted of a neat square about a metre high built of stones with totem poles and cattle skulls on top.

We had got well ahead of the raucous funeral procession and this gave me a chance to interrogate Seraphin, and through him the people we took with us to the graveyard.

'Who let those cattle out right in the middle of the funeral? That nearly ruined everything,' I asked Seraphin.

'Oh no, they were very much part of the funeral,' he replied. 'Those animals were owned by the man who has turned his back. They were driven through the village so that he could say goodbye to them. I think the people also do that so as to show off to the visitors what a wealthy man he was.'

It took me a moment to assimilate that, but then I pressed on. 'Now tell me why the young men carrying the body have gone running all round the place. Why not just carry the body along the track from village to graveyard. Or put it in the coffin? Where is the coffin by the way?'

Seraphin spoke for quite a while to the old men, and then came up with another of his classic answers.

'They run in circles because they want to confuse the spirit. They don't want him to remember how to reach the village from his grave. The village people want the spirit to look after them, but they don't want him coming round the village all the time sticking his nose into everybody's business.' It all made sense once I'd grasped some of the fundamentals.

'So, what's going to happen here now?' I asked Seraphin. It was stupid and naïve of me even to ask, and for answer, he just grinned. We would soon find out because we could hear the cortege approaching.

The Funeral Stakes proved to be a very close race indeed. First, by a short head came the young men with the body. They crashed out of the scrub sweating but still chanting, and with a triumphant flourish they put the body down near to the site of the new grave. Second came a totally exhausted Philip, who had been filming them all the way. A clear length or two behind him came the bullock carts with the coffin and the totem poles. The company of several hundred people straggled in unplaced over the next few minutes.

At this stage the coffin and the body finally came together. I was filming the body being lowered into the coffin, when I became aware of a goat not having a very good day. It was dragged bleating into the middle of the gravesite where it had its throat cut. Almost immediately the man holding the goat ran off with it, and I was totally confused yet again. Men converged on the spot where the goat had been, and feverishly started digging and heaving rocks away from the area.

I filmed all this uncomprehendingly till Seraphin rescued me yet again. 'They must dig the grave where the goat had its throat cut, and they must dig as far down as the goat's blood has gone. On stony ground like this they drag the goat away as quickly as possible so that they don't have to dig too deep.' Once again I was left wondering what we would have done without Seraphin.

As the lid of the coffin was finally put on, the three brothers each took a rock and tapped it three times. I filmed this in ignorance, but learned later that this was the moment when the dead man's nearest relatives told the spirit that he should stay where he was, in the graveyard, and not complicate the lives of the family. Finally rocks were piled on top of the coffin and as the sun set everybody went home. They would complete the building of the grave and the erection of the totem poles over the next few days.

That evening the festivities continued, and we shared in the orgy of meat eating. I have no doubt that all the beef, not to mention all the rum were gone by morning. The dead man had had one hell of a send off, and what we had watched sure beat the solemnity of the usual western funeral.

My understanding of peoples' reactions to death was finally demolished when we reached the centre of Madagascar a couple of months later. This area was settled about fifteen hundred years ago by people from what is today Indonesia, and they brought with them religious practices from that area. Several of these survive today, and the most remarkable to my mind is the practice of re-burial. My initial reaction when I heard about this was that it sounded appalling. To my mind, digging up bodies after they have been buried is sick work for pathologists, the police and crime writers. The chief thing about a funeral, I always thought, was the finality of it. To dig people up again after they have been buried seemed to me like deliberately opening old wounds, re-kindling old sorrows.

The only explanation I managed to read before I left England was that the remains of the dead are wrapped in fresh shrouds as a token of the respect that the living have for their ancestors. I felt sure there more to it than that, but I was simply going to have to wait and see for myself. So from the moment I first arrived in the island, a re-burial ceremony was pretty much top of my personal list of things I wanted to see and film.

Initially the re-burial we filmed was much like the beginning of the crocodile ceremony, with a huge number of people gathering in the courtyard of a house in the village. The most obvious difference was that the band was both bigger and smarter, with all the members wearing a uniform of blue shirts. Those blue shirts seemed to be the only concession the band made to uniformity: otherwise individuality and anarchy seemed the order of the day. They brandished a wondrous array of instruments and played with huge gusto and a total disregard for each other. 'Their solo performances may well have been excellent,' I found myself thinking, 'but the ensemble playing could have done with a little more rehearsal.' Their contribution to the festival atmosphere couldn't be faulted though, and the procession to the graveyard went with a swing, with singing, dancing and lots of excited little children running about.

At the graveyard, work had already started on opening the family tomb. The young men took it in turns to dig, and slowly the huge rocks of the tomb entrance were uncovered. With the arrival of the official party, the older men of the family took over supervision of the work, and eventually the tomb was opened. The music and singing kept up, but there were sober faces in the gathering, and looks of tense expectancy.

Three or four of the older men finally crawled through the opening, taking with them some large pieces of cloth. Gradually the singing quietened down as more and more people pressed round to try and follow events underground. This didn't in the least discourage the band who played on relentlessly and out of tune, but attention was increasingly on the mouth of the tomb.

A surge from the crowd announced that something was happening, so I started filming. The young men at the centre of the throng let out a huge shout as the old men inside the tomb passed out a body-sized bundle. The whole assembly echoed this excited shout as the young men hoisted the bundle above their heads, and pushed their way into the heart of the crowd with their trophy. The band soared to new, un-dreamt of heights, and the whole crowd joined in the excitement.

From the mouth of the tomb came an answering shout, and another body emerged to be borne aloft by young men. Now the two body parties were in competition, each weaving its way through the crowd drawing dancers after it. Yet another shout and there were three congas snaking through the throng.

As with the funeral in the south, information about the re-burial was scarce, but things seemed to be going as expected. Seraphin had managed to learn one key fact, and it had become the cornerstone of our game plan. He had announced with great confidence that three bodies were going to be taken out of the tomb. That was what we were banking on, and here we were with three bodies, so I concentrated on filming the action around one of them. Its mad careering through the crowd slowed and stopped. The body was lowered to the ground, and I realised that the young men had brought it to the feet of a small group of women. They laid the bundle on their laps and tenderly unwrapped it, revealing inside a sticky mess that looked a bit like wet clay with a few bones sticking out of it.

This was the first time I had seen with my own eyes what a human body reverts to after a few years underground, and my initial reaction was one of relief that we weren't all overwhelmed by the putrid stench of decay that I had anticipated. After that, fascination, horror and disgust battled it out for dominance among my thoughts, but I seemed to be pretty much alone there because the faces of the women around me revealed a range of other emotions. The younger ones showed anxiety and just a touch of the shock that I felt, but on the faces of the older women, these things were cut away and what remained was the grief that I should have expected; the emotion that I associate with death. Here were the widow and sisters of the dead man remembering their long dead relative.

The women touched the decayed remains with tenderness, love and sorrow: the emotions I have felt following a death in my own family. The shouting, dancing and music might not quite match the background I expected for such an occasion, but here were reactions I could identify with.

The additional feeling of these mourners was clearly one of pride: probably not only pride in the memory of their dead relative, but also pride that they could do this for him. Seraphin had explained that holding a re-burial ceremony is a great ambition for people in this region. It showed that the dead person was highly respected, and that his memory was still very much alive. It had probably taken years for the family to save the money to hold this ceremony, so today their efforts were being rewarded.

This intimate moment was shattered by a shout from the mouth of the tomb. Another body was carried out, and the singing and dancing were rekindled. This body was followed by another and another. Soon there were bodies everywhere, and the area looked like the scene of a dreadful motorway accident. But the band played on, and people were still dancing, so it became a traffic accident that had failed to dull a surreal pop festival.

Around each body was gathered an intimate scene like the one I was witnessing, with grieving women expressing tender affection. After a while, the group of mourners that I was filming laid out a new piece of cloth, and started to transfer the remains of the body to this new shroud. It was then carefully wrapped up, and for quite a while the mourners sat round the body talking quietly.

It was obvious that these people live with the dead in a way that westerners do not, so the re-burial was not even vaguely like an exhumation. It was a festive reunion when the living could rekindle relationships with their old ancestors, and show those spirits that they are not forgotten but are warmly remembered and honoured. I could understand that motive for the ceremony, but there was clearly something more going on. That second purpose slowly emerged when I asked Seraphin what the women were talking about and he whispered odd translated snatches to me.

What I heard was a synopsis of a soap opera, family happenings over the last few years, and when I heard those details, the second purpose of the reburial dawned on me. As well as honouring the dead, a re-burial also gives the living a chance to update the dead person on events in the family. If the spirits of the ancestors are to look after the living, it is vital for those ancestors to be aware of changes in the world of the living. The living needed to tell their ancestor of the weddings and births that had happened since he turned his back: presumably he already knew about the deaths.

A couple of hours after they had been taken out of the tomb, the bodies, wrapped in their new shrouds, were returned underground rather more sombrely than they had been removed. However, as each body disappeared, the people who had cared for it rejoined the general throng, and there was a steady crescendo in the singing and dancing. By now our contribution to the family party (the inevitable forty litres of rum yet again) made its appearance so events became increasingly excited.

We filmed a bit of this fiesta, but as the light faded we withdrew and at last I could talk to Seraphin. The one fact he had managed to ascertain before the ceremony was that there were to be three bodies involved. Our best estimate was thirteen or fourteen and that seemed more than a slight miscalculation or misunderstanding. He refused to explain, just grinned and hushed my enquiries as he helped get everything packed up. In the car he finally burst out laughing, and explained the mystery of the extra bodies.

'The family told us what they told the authorities; there would be three bodies.'

'Authorities?'

'Yes. You need permission for a re-burial, and you must pay tax. So much per body, and they fiddled the tax man.'

Afterword

As A CHILD I HAD a dream, and to quite an extent it has come true. I dreamt of becoming a wildlife cameraman and for many years that is exactly what I have been. To anybody who is seriously interested in animals, my job is bliss. It costs so much to send a cameraman off filming that the producer makes damn sure you go to the best possible place to film what is wanted. He, or now more usually she, also sends you at the best possible time, and with the assistance of the best possible advisors. As a result I have met some fascinating people and I have been able to see more wildlife, and more exciting wildlife, than I had even heard of as a child.

The job has often taken me beyond merely seeing the most wonderful animals because I have often been able to interact with them. So I have had terrific fun manipulating animals such as vultures in Kenya or anacondas in Venezuela. I have adored meeting and getting close to enchanting creatures like gibbons and gorillas. And (chiefly in hindsight) I have revelled in the excitement of getting rather too close to animals such as polar bears, lions and caiman. So I don't want anybody to get me wrong about this: it's a great job.

But my dream was not exclusively about giving myself an exciting and interesting life: I also wanted to save the world. I admit that I hadn't thought out the business of saving the world in great detail, but it was very much part of my childhood ambition. I haven't referred to it much because that part of my dream hasn't really come true.

As a teenager, I learned about ecology and saw little but impending doom and disaster. I know that teenagers tend to view the world that way, but I was very serious about it and studied it in some depth. I saw desertification, deforestation, eutrophication of freshwater and many other –ations, but hovering above all of them was the big one – human population. I saw this last as the greatest danger, so I had a poster on my wall showing the Pope with the caption, 'Why won't he preach what he practices?'

I pinned my hopes on educating people, arguing that once everybody knew as much about these problems as I did (I was a modest youth), they would do something about them. The wildlife films that I planned to make for television would be my contribution to the world's education. In the light of my experience though, I'm not quite sure how much I have been helping to save the world, and I'm even starting to wonder whether being a cameraman puts me on the side of the good guys at all.

We cameramen go jetting off to see and film the finest wildlife sites (and sights) in the world. The worry is that we then then put the images we collect onto television screens, and pat ourselves on the back saying that we've done our bit. Unfortunately, when people see some wonderful animal or place on television, what they think is not so much 'I must do everything possible to save that', they think something more along the lines of 'I want to go there and see that'.

And who am I to blame them? That's how I react, in fact it's one of the huge attractions of the job. So it's not good enough for me to say that I should be paid to go off to the Arctic to see and film polar bears, but nobody else should be allowed to go there. That would be special pleading, which is always suspect. Unfortunately, the case for me going to the Arctic may be worse than that because, as a result of me going and filming polar bears, more and more people seem to want to go there and see them too. Tragically the Arctic is such a fragile place that all those visitors are doing irreparable damage, so if my efforts encourage people to go there, perhaps everybody should be allowed to go there except me.

On really bad days, I see the whole wildlife film industry as producing nothing more valuable than a massive stream of free advertising for the travel industry, and the travel industry is one of the most destructive in the world.

I heard only the other day that there is a hole a mile wide in the ice at the North Pole. If anything could make my point this is it, because the scientist who reported this horrific find discovered it while lecturing on board one of the Russian nuclear icebreakers, *Yamal*, the one that brought Philip and me home from Franz Joseph Land.

And what, you may ask, was *Yamal* doing at the North Pole? It was taking a group of tourists there, as it had been doing when I was aboard. It doesn't seem too far-fetched to imagine that icebreakers smashing their way to the North Pole every couple of weeks might have contributed to the break up of the ice there. The destructive power of tourism is at work. 'See Polar bears', 'Swim at the Pole' followed by 'a barbecue on the ice'; these are the leading attractions of the polar tours. The people I met on board felt they had achieved a lifelong ambition when they did these things, but I rather doubt they would even have had those ambitions in the first place if they had never seen film of the Arctic and its bears. It could be that the film I shot has made a significant contribution to the hole in the Arctic ice. On good days I realise that I am simply not that significant, and I shouldn't try to take sole responsibility for global warming.

The other down side to the fulfilment of my ambition is on a rather more modest scale than saving the world, but it is important to me. Heading off and spending three or four months in the Arctic filming polar bears is very exciting, but it does put the odd strain on family life. It is only because I was lucky enough to marry a strong and understanding girl that I still have a wife today.

One example will show what I mean. A couple of days before I left for Franz Joseph Land, my elder daughter, Emma, finished her exams at school, so she got the results while I was away. We had a satellite phone with us, and, against all the odds, I managed to get through on the day the results came out.

'Hello love. How did you get on?'

'Hello Dad. It's amazing. I got seven As and three Bs.'

'Oh wow. That's wonderful. Well done. You really deserved it. Terrific. Super.' I went on like that for a while, but Emma missed it all. She didn't know about the pauses between messages on the satellite phone, so having told me her wonderful news, all she heard was Arctic silence. So she turned to Caroline and said, 'I think he's disappointed.' Caroline heard my ecstatic words, and had to console a weeping Emma. Before I could talk directly to Emma again, I had to break off the call because there was a bear heading purposefully towards me, so we all spent the next weeks feeling terrible about each other.

Oscar Wilde wrote, 'There is only one thing worse than not getting what you want, and that is getting it.' There is no way I could say that about being a wildlife cameraman, but it isn't quite what I expected.

Indeed, as a cameraman, things never seem to turn out quite as I expect. Most of the incidents recounted in this book support that fact, but one final experience underlines it. While I was working in Thailand filming my favourite animals, gibbons, an opportunity presented itself out of the blue, to include an elephant in the programme, and I wasn't about to pass it up. Peaw, our local fixer, spotted a bull elephant walking along a river just near to the little cafe we were heading for. Ignoring Peaw's muttered comment of 'Take care', I picked up the camera and found the elephant where it had stopped to eat some banana trees just behind the cafe.

There's something stupidly comfortable about elephants. They look so familiar, slow and gentle, and down the viewfinder he looked totally benign. I found myself getting closer and closer to this one buoyed up by my camera courage. I need a shot of his head, I told myself. A shot of just his trunk might be useful. A tight shot of his eye would be nice. I inched closer till I was less than fifteen metres from him, filming away and thoroughly pleased with myself.

That was when he realised I was there and that I was too close for his comfort. He put his ears forward, raised his trunk and came for me. In an instant he switched from being an image of a loveable dependable giant down the viewfinder to a huge and very real threat. He was moving fast, and he was obviously very angry with me. It was a bad moment but I grabbed the camera and ran for the car. I could hear him behind me as I ran, but the cafe tables must have slowed him down more than me because I made it to the car just ahead of him. Peaw had the door open and the engine running, so off we went.

I was badly shaken, but a bit elated to have got away. When I calmed down enough to be aware of what was going on, I realised that Peaw was driving us to the little museum that the park authorities had set up.

'I want to show you something,' he said. He led me to a photo on the wall. In the picture there was a Buddhist monk in his saffron robe holding his hand up like a policeman stopping traffic. About a metre away from the raised hand was an elephant.

'When a monk approaches enlightenment he can control wild animals,' said Peaw, 'to control an elephant is the greatest test. Now read the caption.'

Under the picture was written: 'Seni Tean, two seconds before his death.'

'That is the elephant you were filming just now,' said Peaw. 'Please be more careful.'